AF026

MASSIMILIANO AFIERO

AXIS FORCES 26

WW2 AXIS FORCES

The Axis Forces 026 ENG - First edition February 2025 by Luca Cristini Editor for the brand Soldiershop
Cover & Art Design by soldiershop factory. ISBN code: 9791255892144
Copyright © 2025 Luca Cristini Editore (BG) ITALY. No part of this publication may be reproduced, stored in a retrieval system or transmitted by any form or by any means, electronic, recording or otherwise without the prior permission in writing from the publishers. The publisher remains to disposition of the possible having right for all the doubtful sources images or not identifies. Visit www.soldiershop.com to read more about all our books and to buy them.

Direzione e redazione: Via San Giorgio, 11 – 80021 AFRAGOLA (NA) -ITALY
Caporedattore: Massimiliano Afiero
Email: maxafiero@libero.it – Sito web: www.maxafiero.it

Redaction

Tomasz Borowski, Grégory Bouysse, Stefano Canavassi, Carlos Caballero Jurado, Rene Chavez, Gary Costello, Paolo Crippa, Carlo Cucut, Antonio Guerra, Lars Larsen, Christophe Leguérandais, Eduardo M. Gil Martínez, Michael D. Miller, Peter Mooney, Péter Mujzer, Ken Niewiarowicz, Erik Norling, Raphael Riccio, Marc Rikmenspoel, Guido Ronconi, Hugh Page Taylor, Charles Trang, Sergio Volpe

Editorial

Finally, we are pleased to present the first issue of 2025, and we sincerely apologize to our readers for the long and unexpected delay. Unfortunately, due to various reasons, we have lost some of our key contributors who, occupied with other professional commitments, were no longer able to assist us. This sudden change forced us to reorganize the entire editorial planning of the magazine. With this issue, we hope to embark on a new chapter and, most importantly, to ensure a much more regular publication schedule moving forward.
The new articles have been carefully selected, with a continued focus on the Axis forces and, in particular, on the foreign volunteer formations that fought alongside the German and Italian military. In the future, we aim to explore new and lesser-known topics, shedding light on the more obscure but equally fascinating volunteer units from a historical-military perspective. As always, we invite all readers to share their comments and suggestions, as your feedback is invaluable in helping us improve the content of the magazine together.
Now, let's delve into the contents of this new issue: we begin with an article dedicated to the SS-Jagdverbände, the special forces of the Waffen-SS. This is followed by a biography of Latvian volunteer Miervaldis Adamson. Next, we explore the Tagliamento Legion of the Italian Social Republic, the 162nd Turkestan Division, the Debica Battalion of the Italian SS Legion, and we conclude with another biography, this time of Danish volunteer Egon Christophersen. We wish you all an enjoyable read and look forward to seeing you in the next issue.

The Axis Forces is a publication dedicated exclusively to historical-military topics. It does not seek to glorify any political ideology, past or present, nor does it endorse any political regime of the previous century or any form of racism.

Contents

SS-Jagdverbande di Charles Trang	Pag. 2
Waffen-Hauptsturmführer Miervaldis Adamsons by Cesare Veronesi	Pag. 28
1ª Legione d'Assalto "Tagliamento" 1943 – 1945 by Paolo Crippa	Pag. 33
The 162. (Turk.) Infanterie-Division di Danilo Morisco	Pag. 44
The battalion SS 'Debica' by Leonardo Sandri	Pag. 69
SS-Unterscharführer Egon Christophersen by Antonio Guerra	Pag. 93

Tiger tank and *Waffen-SS* soldiers on the streets of Budapest, October 1944.

SS-Jagdverbande

by Charles Trang

Walter Schellenberg and Otto Skorzeny.

The 'Friedenthal Sonderverband' and the liberation of Mussolini

Although dependent on the *SD-Ausland* headed by *SS-Brigdf.* Walter Schellenberg, the *SS-Jagdverbände*, during the last year of the war, were engaged in missions initially reserved for units of the *'Brandenburg'* division. Their leader was Otto Skorzeny, a Viennese engineer transferred from a *Luftwaffe* transmission regiment to the SS on 21 February 1940. After a brief move to the *Leibstandarte*, Skorzeny was transferred to the *'Germania'* regiment, then after the French campaign of 1940, he moved to the artillery regiment of the *SS-Verfügungsdivision*. He served in the *II.Abteilung* in the position of chief for vehicle maintenance (TFK). In the autumn, he replaced *SS-Stubaf.* Schäffer by taking over the entire technical service of the artillery regiment. In January 1942, suffering from liver colic, he had to be evacuated and then joined the *Leibstandarte* depot battalion in Berlin-Lichterfelde. Promoted *SS-Hauptsturmführer*, he was transferred to the armoured regiment of the *SS-Panzergrenadier-Division 'Totenkopf'*, but an attack of dysentery made him unfit for the front line. In April 1943, he was assigned to *SD-Ausland*'s 'S' (*Schule*) service, which depended on the *RSiHA*. The *SD-Ausland* was the foreign department of the Security Service. This department was on the verge of being transformed into an espionage centre and this would have put it in competition with Admiral Canaris' *Abwehr*. And so, the *SD-Ausland* created a battalion (*SS-Bataillon 'Oranienburg'*) to be engaged in special missions of the same type as those carried out by the *Abwehr*'s *Brandenburg* commandos. The staff of this new unit, whose command was assigned to *SS-Hstuf.* Skorzeny, quartered in Friedenthal Castle. This battalion was renamed *SS-Jagdverbande 502* and comprised a grenadier company, a heavy company and a transport unit. On 25 July 1943, Skorzeny was summoned to the Wolf's Lair, where Hitler entrusted him with the mission of liberating the Duce. The next day, he arrived in Italy in the company of General Student, passing himself off as his commanding officer.

General Kurt Student gives the last orders to Otto Skorzeny and his men before the action on the Gran Sasso.

About fifty men, led by *SS-Hstuf*. Menzel (*Chef 1.Kommando/SS-Jagdverband 502*), the *SS-Ostuf*. Radl (*Btl.-Adjutant*) and the *SS-Ustuf*. Schwerdt and Warger, reached him on the 27th. The SS had exchanged their outfits for *Luftwaffe* uniforms. After a difficult search, Skorzeny managed to locate the place where the Duce was imprisoned. The latter was locked up in a winter sports hotel at the foot of the Gran Sasso mountain in the Campo Imperatore region of the Abruzzo Apennines. It was necessary to act quickly because the Italians had capitulated on 8 September. On the 12th, ninety paratroopers from the *1st Fallschirmjäger-Division* and 17 from *SS-Jagdverband 502* (still called *Bataillon 'Friedenthal'*) boarded *DFS 230* gliders at Pratica di Mare airfield. With Skorzeny were *Oberleutnant* Berlepsch (of the *Luftwaffe*), *SS-Hstuf*. Menzel and the *SS-Ustuf*. Schwerdt and Warger. With them also Carabinieri General Soletti: his presence was initially intended to avoid unnecessary bloodshed. In addition, the paratrooper battalion 'Mors' was to attack from the Assergi valley. Navigational errors and take-off problems reduced the commando's strength to seventy men. After a rather difficult landing, the SS and paratroopers quickly neutralised the Italian garrison and liberated Mussolini.

Pictured left gliders and German paratroopers on the Gran Sasso, September 1943. Right one of the *Fallschirmjäger* who took part in the operation on the Gran Sasso, 1943.

Otto Skorzeny with German and Italian soldiers immediately after the liberation of Mussolini, 1943.

The Duce then left the Gran Sasso and was taken to Vienna in the company of Skorzeny aboard a *Fieseler Storch*. The operation was a great success. For this action, Skozeny was promoted to *SS-Sturmbannführer* and decorated with the Knight's Cross. Taking advantage of this situation, *SS-Jagdverband 502* was reinforced and now comprised three motorised companies and a staff company. New officers joined the unit; among them was *SS-Ostuf*. Adrian von Fölkersam, recently transferred from the *'Brandenburg'* division, with which he had been decorated with the Knight's Cross. Skorzeny made him his chief of staff. Between October and November 1943, enlistments were increased and training resumed.

The SS-Stubaf. Otto Skorzeny decorated with the Knight's Cross during an official ceremony.

Otto Skorzeny with his men at the Friedenthal camp.

At the end of November, Skorzeny arrived in Paris with a company of his battalion. The orders were to surround Vichy and stand ready to kidnap Marshal Pétain! Two police battalions, supplied by *SS-Gruf.* Oberg, were placed under his command. In the end, the operation was called off on 20 December 1943.

In February 1944, the *SD-Ausland* was merged with the *Abwehr*, whose leader, Admiral Canaris, had been forced to resign. Friedenthal's SS was also instructed on *V1s* and human torpedoes. But no new operation was launched. On 17 April 1944, the *Sonderverband z.b.V. 'Friedenthal'* was renamed, becoming *SS-Jäger-Bataillon 502* (*SS-FHA, Amt II Org.Abt.Ia/II, Tgb.Nr.993/44 g.Kdos*). The unit then took on a new structure:

Stab, Stabs-Kp.

1.-3.Schützen-Kp.(mot.)
Legionärs-Kp.(mot.)

It should be noted that the battalion was now subordinate to the *SS-FHA* and thus belonged to the *Waffen-SS*. The first mission of the year did not arrive until 20 July 1944: a company from the battalion was sent to Berlin to protect the buildings of *Amt VI*.

Otto Skorzeny in Berlin, 20 July 1944.

It later reached the headquarters of the War Ministry to reinforce the 'Remer' battalion. Once the plot against Hitler was resolved, Skorzeny's men returned to Friedenthal.

At the end of July, Skorzeny's staff was as follows:

<u>Adjutant</u>: *SS-Hauptsturmführer* Radl
<u>Chef d.Stabes</u>: *SS-Hstuf.* von Fölkersam
<u>Ia</u>: *SS-Hauptsturmführer* Hunke
<u>Ib</u>: *SS-Hauptsturmführer* Gerhardt
<u>Ic</u>: *SS-Ostuf.* Riedl, poi *SS-Ostuf.* Graf
<u>IIa</u>: *SS-Obersturmführer* Gallent
<u>IIb</u>: *SS-Hauptsturmführer* Weiss
<u>III</u>: *SS-Obersturmführer* Pinder
<u>IVa</u>: *SS-Hauptsturmführer* Urbanek
<u>IVb</u>: *SS-Hauptsturmführer* Dr Wetz
<u>V</u>: *SS-Obersturmführer* Weber
<u>VI</u>: *SS-Standartenführer* Bayer

Operation Panzerfaust

At the end of the summer of 1944, with the Soviets now fighting on Hungarian soil, the regent, Nicolas Horthy, attempted through secret talks to obtain a separate peace with them. However, the Germans did not stand by and Skorzeny received orders to take over the Burgberg in Budapest, the seat of the Hungarian government, if Horthy would betray the German-Hungarian alliance. For this operation, code-named *'Panzerfaust'*, Skorzeny had at his disposal the *SS-Jagdverband Mitte* (the former *SS-Jagdverband 502*), a company of *SS-Fallschirmjäger 600*, about 200 *Luftwaffe* parachutists, 700 trainee officers from the Wiener-Neustadt school and a company of *schw.Pz.Abt.503* equipped with *Königstiger*. The *SS-Hstuf.* von Fölkersam and the *SS-Ustuf.* Ostafel (*Ord.-Offz.*) quickly reached Budapest where they made contact with the German garrison in the city. Skorzeny's units quartered in the suburbs of Budapest at the beginning of October.

Waffen-SS **units and Royal Tiger tanks on the streets of Budapest, 1944.**

On the 15th, a company of the *SS-Jagdverband 'Mitte'* provided protection for the SD policemen who had come to pick up the regent's son, Niklas Horthy, during his meeting with Tito's emissaries. On the same day, the regent announced on the radio that he had concluded a preliminary agreement for an armistice with the Soviets. By this time, Hungary was in danger of switching sides to the Allies. Operation *Panzerfaust* was therefore launched. The *22nd SS-Freiwilligen-Kavallerie-Division* immediately occupied all key points of the Hungarian capital. The Germans thus managed to control almost all of Budapest, except for the *Burgberg*, the hill with the government castle. Horthy was summoned to cancel the proposed armistice. The next day, Skorzeny went on the attack.

A Tiger bursts into the *Burgberg*.

SS soldiers in Buda Castle, October 1944.

German units on the streets of Budapest, 1944.

While the SS parachute company arrived at the Ministry of the Interior via the Chain Bridge and the *1.Kp./SS-Jagdverband 'Mitte'* (*SS-Ostuf.* Hunke) headed towards the castle from the west, the bulk of the forces entered the *Burgberg* via the Vienna Gate. The Hungarians offered no resistance. In less than thirty minutes, the *Burgberg* was neutralised. There were only seven casualties: four Germans and three Hungarians. Regent Horthy while trying to reach the *SS-Gruf.* Karl von Pfeffer-Wildenbruch, was arrested and taken to Hirschberg Castle.

Integration of the Brandenburg commandos into the Waffen-SS

On 4 October 1944, the *SS-FHA* issued the order to integrate the *Brandenburg commandos*, with their men and equipment, into the *Waffen-SS*[1]. These were the following units:

Verbindungsstab West mit Streifkorps Südfrankreich, Nordfrankreich, Belgien
Streifkorpseinsatzgruppe Italien
Streifkorps Kroatien (Wehrwirtschaftsstab 85)
Streifkorps Rumänien, Siebenbürgen
Streifkorps Einsatzgruppe Slowakei
Streifkorps Einsatzgruppe Baltikum

Photo left, Budapest, Buda Castle, October 1944: *SS-Stubaf.* Otto Skorzeny, with *SS-Hstuf.* Adrian von Fölkersam and *SS-Ostuf.* Walter Girg. On the right, Skorzeny again in Buda.

Otto Skorzeny with Adolf Hitler.

Their reorganisation within *the SS-Jagdverbände* was left to the *SS-Stubaf.* Otto Skorzeny. These units now comprised the following elements:

Führungsstab and Stabs-Kp.(mot.) SS-Jagdverbände
Versorgungs-Kp. (t.Bewegl.mot.) SS-Jagdverbände
Eins.Beauftr. SS-Jagdverbände
Stab e Ausb.Kp. Sondereinsatz-Abt. SS-Jagdverbände
Funkschule SS-Jagdverbände
Kampfschule SS-Jagdverbände
SS-Jäger-Bataillon 'Nordwest'
SS-Jäger-Bataillon 'Südwest'
SS-Jäger-Bataillon 'Südost'
SS-Jäger-Bataillon 'Ost'

Formation of the Panzer-Brigade 150

While preparing his counter-offensive in the Ardennes, Hitler decided that he needed a special unit to conquer the bridges over the Meuse. This special unit, fully equipped with American equipment and with its men in American uniforms, was to take advantage of the surprise effect and panic created by the initial penetration of the attack to move towards the Meuse by posing as a retreating column. This idea was not entirely new.

SS-Stubaf. Otto Skorzeny.

Already in Russia, the *Brandenburg commandos* had used this ruse successfully. To lead the mission, Hitler chose Skorzeny. He received him in Rastenburg on 22nd October. Promoted *SS-Obersturmbannführer*, Skorzeny had the main lines of his mission explained to him. He had only five weeks to form his unit, which he christened *Panzer-Brigade 150*. On 25 October, he sent his plans to General Jodl with a complete list of the equipment he needed. He thus envisaged that his brigade should comprise 3,300 men divided into three battalions and logistical units. He was promised unlimited support.

Left, *Panzerbrigade* men in enemy uniforms and right with an *M3 Half Track.*

On the same day, the OKW issued its orders to find recruits who could speak English and knew American 'slang'. However, from the moment of its initial preparation, the Allies received all the details of the operation, as confirmed by a report from the staff of the *1st Canadian Army*. Furthermore, Skorzeny found it very difficult to find American equipment and suitable recruits for his brigade. The material existed, but the units that possessed it were reluctant to hand it over.

German motorised units on the eve of the counter-offensive in the Ardennes, December 1944.

A German soldier on the Western Front, 1944.

On 9 November, the *OB West* was assigned the mission to find 15 tanks, 20 armoured cars, 20 towed artillery pieces, 100 jeeps, 40 motorbikes and 120 trucks as well as American and British uniforms. This requisition (code name: *'Rabenhügel'*) was shared between the three army groups, which included the *OB West*. This material was to be taken to Grafenwöhr where the Brigade was being formed. With little material available, it had to be supplemented with German equipment: and so it was that *Panther* and *StuGs* were repainted in olive green with white 'American' stars.

The Axis Forces

Five *Panthers* were transformed into American M-10 tank fighters! As of 5 November 1944, the 'theoretical' order of battle of the Skorzeny Armoured Brigade was as follows:

- *Brigade Stab*
- *Aufklärungs-Zug*
- *Nachrichten-Zug*
- *I./Kampfabteilung 2150*
  Stab mit Nachrichten-Zug
  1.(Pz.)Kp. (22 PzKpfw.V)
  2.(Pz.Gren.)Kp. (SPW)
  3.(Pz.Sp.)Kp. (18 Pz.Sp.Wg.)
  4. – 7.(Schtz.)Kp. (mot.)
  8.(Flak)Kp. (6 Flak 8,8 cm e 3 Flak 2 cm)
- *II./Kampfabteilung 2150*
  Stab mit Nachrichten-Zug
  9.(StuG)Kp. (14 StuG.III)
  10.(Pz.Sp.)Kp. (16 Pz.Sp.Wg.)
  11.-14.(Schtz.)Kp. (mot.)
  15.(Flak)Kp. (6 Flak 8,8 cm e 3 Flak 2 cm)
- *Pionier-Kp.2150*
- *Artillerie-Batterie 2150 (6 le.FH10,5cm)*
- *Brücko 2150 (60t)*

German soldiers in the Ardennes, 1945.

However, the Brigade's actual strength was less. Only 5 *PzKpfw.V* were delivered on 19 November, 5 *StuG.III* and 6 armoured cars on the 24th and 6 *m.SPW* on the 27th. Of the 150 vehicles and 198 trucks requested, 57 and 74 arrived respectively. In addition, a third of the vehicles complained of various breakdowns and were in need of repair. The only two *Shermans* recovered were also non-operational. Russian and Polish equipment, absolutely unusable for this operation, was, however, found in considerable quantities. There were also 1,500 American helmets missing and the letters 'KG' (*Kriegsgefangener*, prisoner of war) were painted on most of the recovered uniforms. In addition, many uniforms were of the summer type. As for the recruits, the situation was equally catastrophic. Skorzeny classified his men into several categories: the first, made up of men who spoke perfect English and knew American 'slang', comprised only ten soldiers, mostly sailors; the second, made up of about thirty men, who spoke perfect English but did not know American 'slang'; the third, comprised of about 120 men, who could speak English correctly; and the fourth, of 200 men, who had learnt English at school. The rest of the recruits could only say *'Yes'*. Faced with this situation, Skorzeny was forced to form a commando with 150 men who knew English well. Grouped within the *Einheit Stielau* and placed under the orders of

SS-Hstuf. Stielau, they were quickly trained for their mission: none of them had experience with commando and sabotage operations.

German officers study maps on the eve of the offensive, December 1944.

Directions before the attack, 1944.

The *Einheit Stielau* was then formed into demolition groups, consisting of 5-6 men, which were to sabotage bridges, fuel and ammunition depots, into reconnaissance groups, consisting of 3-4 men, which were to infiltrate between the American lines to obtain information on enemy movements and sow panic in their rear lines, and finally into leading groups, consisting of 3-4 men, with the mission of disrupting American communications by cutting telephone lines, destroying radio stations and issuing false orders. The bulk of the personnel consisted of one company of the *SS-Jagdverband 'Mitte'*, two of the *SS-Fallschirmjäger-Bataillon 600*, two paratrooper battalions initially attached to the *Sonderverband 'Jungwirth'* (*Kampfgeschwader 200*) and the *7.Pz.Gren.Kp.(gep.)*. The tank crews came from *I./Pz.Rgt.11*, those of the armoured cars from *1.Kp./Pz.Aufkl.-Abt.190* and *1.Kp./Pz.Aufkl.-Abt.2*, those of the assault guns from the *1.Kp./s.Pz.Jg.-Abt.655*, while the artillerymen came from the *Artillerie-Abteilung 1./40* and their howitzers from the *Führer-Grenadier-Brigade*. The staff of *Panzer-Brigade 150* was formed from that of *Panzer-Brigade 108* and those of the two battalions with personnel from Panzer-Brigade 10 and *Panzer-Brigade 113*. With the genius specialists and logistics units, the brigade grew to about 2,500 men, of which 500 were from the *Waffen-SS* and 800 from the *Luftwaffe*.

Panther and German trucks on the march, 1944.

An *'M10' Panther* from *Kampfgruppe X*.

It was eventually restructured into three tactical groupings, each comprising a staff, three infantry companies, two motorised infantry platoons, two anti-tank platoons, two heavy mortar platoons, a pioneer platoon, a transmission platoon and a repair shop:

- *Kampfgruppe X* (*SS-Ostubaf.* Hardieck) with the 5 *PzKpfw.V*
- *Kampfgruppe Y* (*Hauptmann* Scherf) with the 5 *StuG.III*
- *Kampfgruppe Z* (*Oberstleutnant* Wolf)

The Axis Forces

Adrian von Fölkersam with the *Ritterkreuz*.

German soldiers in the Ardennes, 1944.

Training began in Grafenwöhr under the direction of the *SS-Ostubaf*. Hardieck. It was not until 10 December that the Brigade officers were informed of the details of their mission: they were to capture at least two bridges over the Meuse at Huy, Amay and Andenne. The unit was to go into action as soon as the armoured divisions reached the Hautes Fagnes[2]. Attacking at night, the Brigade was to reach its objectives in less than six hours.

Operation Greif

On 14 December, Dr Solar's units (codenamed Skorzeny) left Wahn and regrouped near Münstereifel. In the afternoon of the 16th, the Brigade set off following the divisions of the *I.SS-Pz.Korps*. In the early hours of the attack, Willi Hardieck was killed after stepping on a mine. It was Skorzeny's aide Adrian von Fölkersam who replaced him in command of *Kampfgruppe X*. Unfortunately for the Germans, the *I.SS-Pz.Korps* was stuck. Operation *Greif* could practically be considered to have already failed. Moreover, the details of the operation were now known to the Americans after documents concerning it in the hands of the *62nd VGD* were captured by the *7th US AD*. Skorzeny then proposed to Sepp Dietrich to commit the Brigade as assault troops and he agreed. *Panzer-Brigade 150* was then ordered to take the Malmedy position on 21 December, to disengage *Kampfgruppe Peiper*. Thus on 20 December, *Kampfgruppen X* and *Y* regrouped near Ligneuville while *Kampfgruppe Z* was held in reserve. Without artillery support and no surprise effect, after one of the soldiers had been captured the day before, the Brigade had no chance of conquering Malmedy. On 21 December, *Kampfgruppe Y*'s attack was repulsed by a terrible artillery barrage. *Kampfgruppe X* was instead blocked on the *Warche* river. The next day, *Kampfgruppe Y* tried again, but again unsuccessfully, to break through from the east.

Waffen-SS soldiers pass a destroyed American column, December 1944.

The only *Panther 'M10'* of *Kampfgruppe X* to reach the northern bank of the Amblève River at Malmedy. He was blocked fifty metres from the bridge by a *Bazooka* shell that hit him in the engine compartment.

In the afternoon, American pioneers blew up the railway bridge on *Route Nationale 32*, thus blocking the road west of Malmedy, as well as the one on the road to *La Falize*. The bridge over the *Warche* was also destroyed. The various elements of *Panzer-Brigade 150* remained on the line until 28 December, only to be taken over by the units of the *18th Volks-Grenadier-Division*. The unit was then transferred to Schlierbach east of Saint-Vith, where it was taken by train in the direction of Grafenwöhr. Here, it was disbanded and its men were sent back to their original units. Its losses amounted to about 15% of the committed troops at the beginning of the offensive.

Another abandoned *Panther M10* near the village of La Falize.

An 'American' *StuG.III* abandoned at Géromond.

The commandos of the Einheit Stielau

In the early days of *'Wacht am Rhein'*, Skorzeny sent four squads of reconnaissance commandos and two squads of demolition *commandos* between the American lines, while one squad of *commandos* was engaged with each of the following units:

- 1.SS-Panzerdivision 'LSSAH'
- 12.SS-Panzerdivision 'Hitlerjugend'
- 12.Volksgrenadier-Division
- Kampfgruppen X, Y and Z

These squads *of commandos* achieved incredible successes, considering their small numbers. They created chaos and confusion among the American lines, cutting lines of communication, diverting units from their destinations. The psychological impact was such that the Americans began to see enemy infiltrators and saboteurs everywhere. At the end of the operations, eighteen men of the *Einheit Stielau* were captured, court-martialled at Henri-Chapelle and executed.

Left, the tragic end of an *Einheit Stielau* team: a destroyed Jeep and a member of the unit killed, December 1944. On the right, the capture of a member of the same unit.

Otto Skorzeny in the Schwedt sector.

The Schwedt bridgehead

Once the operations in the Ardennes were over, on 30 January 1945, Skorzeny was ordered to take command of the troops that were to establish a bridgehead at Schwedt am Oder. This was to serve as a base for a later counter-attack. For this mission, Skorzeny had at his disposal the *SS-Jagdverband 'Nordwest'*, whose personnel included a company, part of the *SS-Jagdverband 'Mitte'* and the *SS-Fallsch.Jg.-Btl.600*. It should be noted that after 10 November 1944, *SS-Fallsch.Jg.Btl.600* and *SS-Fallsch.Jg.Ausb.Kp.* were part of the *SS-Jagdverbände* (*SS-FHA, Amt II Org.Abt.Ia/II, Tgb.Nr.4214/44 g.kdos*). The convoys arrived in Schwedt on 31 January 1945. The local garrison comprised 150 non-commissioned officers and aspirants from an engineer school and 500 senior and junior members of a *Volksturm* battalion. Some isolates and fugitives, cut off from their units, were enlisted for the defence of the bridgehead. The numerous refugees were channelled westwards, while an outpost was established at Königsberg-Neumark with the *3.Kp./SS-Fallsch.Jg.-Btl.600* (*SS-Ostuf.* Markus). A new battalion of the *Volksturm* militia, made up of Hamburg dockers and *Luftwaffe* personnel, arrived to reinforce the defensive device. Skorzeny organised a small staff under the responsibility of *Oberstleutnant* Walther, a veteran of the *'Brandenburg'* division. Fortifications, forming an arc of between 5 and 6 kilometres in radius, were quickly formed on the eastern bank of the Oder. Three *Flak* groups, equipped with 88 and 105 cannons, constituted the heavy armament of the

'Schwedt' division (also called *Sonderverband 'Skorzeny'*), which now comprised 12,000 men thanks to the arrival of a cavalry squadron and Romanian volunteers from the *Waffen-SS*. Fifteen *Pak 40s* (7.5 cm), recovered from a factory south of the city, also reinforced the defensive potential.

German anti-aircraft artillery on the Oder front, February 1945.

Defence position on the Schwedt bridgehead.

In addition, the *Heeres-StuG-Brigade 210* (*Major* Langel) was made available to the 'division'. Coming from Szczecin, it comprised 31 *StuG.IVs* fresh from the factory. On 8 February, the Soviets attacked the positions of Grabow and Hausberg. They lost thirteen tanks during the clashes with the assault guns of the *'Kohler'* and *'Naumann'* batteries. The position of Johannisgrund was recaptured by the *2.Kp./SS-Fallsch.Jg.-Btl.600* (*SS-Ostuf.* Scheu) and some elements of the *SS-Jagdverband 'Mitte'* (*SS-Hstuf.* Fucker). Between 9 and 10 February, the Soviets intensified their pressure. German losses were heavy, but the German bridgehead continued to resist. The latter was reinforced by an assault company from Friedenthal (*SS-Sturm-Kp.*) under the orders of *SS-Ostuf.* Schwerdt and a company of sharpshooters (*SS-Scharfschützen-Kp.*) led by *SS-Ostuf.*

Wisler.

SS-Fallschirmjäger **on the Schwedt bridgehead, 1945.**

SS-Fallschirmjäger **and Soviet tank destroyed.**

On 17 February, the Soviets resumed their offensive, concentrating their efforts in front of Nipperwiese, in the northern sector of the bridgehead. This village was defended by the bulk of the *SS-Jagdverband 'Nordwest'* and the airborne battalion (initially intended to serve within the *Fallschirm-Panzergrenadier-Division 'Hermann Göring'*). These units held their positions for six days, destroying several dozen enemy tanks. At the end of the month, the *3.Kp./SS-Fallsch.Jg.-Btl.600* was forced to abandon the Königsberg-Neumark outpost. The town's defenders fell back to the main line of resistance. The fighting continued to get fiercer and fiercer. A quick counter-attack allowed the village of Hanseberg, south of Schwedt, to be retaken. However, this local success no longer counted for anything. The bridgehead, which was tactically dependent on the *SS-Oder-Korps* (*SS-Ogruf.* von dem Bach), no longer represented a strategic interest in the overall framework of the German defence system and therefore the order came to evacuate it. Skorzeny was called to Friedenthal on 1 March 1945. The *SS-Jagdverbände* were now engaged in combat as mere infantry units until the end of the war.

Otto Skorzeny in conversation with the *SS-Hstuf*. Milius in Schwedt, 1945.

SS-Fallschirmjäger inspect a destroyed Soviet tank.

SS-Jagdverband 'Mitte'

The *SS-Jagdverband 'Mitte'* was formed from *SS-Jagdverband 502* in October 1944. The new unit, under the orders of *SS-Hstuf.* Fucker, comprised a staff company, three German companies, three legionnaire companies and a heavy weapons company. In December, the *5.Kompanie*, with 175 men, participated in the offensive in the Ardennes as part of *Panzer-Brigade 150*. The survivors of the company then reached Friedenthal in January 1945. The *SS-Jagdverband 'Mitte'* then fought on the Schwedt bridgehead from 1 February to 3 March and then on the Zehden bridgehead as part of *Kampfgruppe Solar* from 3 to 28 March 1945. Left with only two companies, comprising a total of 250 men, the unit arrived in Austria with Skorzeny to organise the famous 'Alpine Redoubt'. It settled in Linz, where the remnants of the *SS-Jagdverbände 'Südwest'* and *'Südost'* also arrived. The unit capitulated in May 1945.

The Axis Forces

March 1945, Oder front: Otto Skorzeny handing over the Badge for tank destroyer with individual weapons to elements of his combat group, comprising elements of the army and *Waffen-SS*.

Another photo of the Badge presentation ceremony.

Members of *Einsatzgruppe 'Slowakei'* during an action.

SS-Jagdverband 'Südost'

The *SS-Jagdverband 'Südost'* was formed from the *Streifkorps 'Karpaten'* of the Brandenburg *commandos*. It was led by *Major* Auch, former commander of the battalion of legionnaires who had fought against the French partisans in the Vercors. The unit comprised two companies, *Einsatzgruppe 'Slowakei'* and *Einsatzgruppe 'Rumänien'* (under the orders of *W- Stubaf.* Toba with *SS-Stubaf.* Benesch as liaison officer) which had been formed in August 1944. The personnel of the Slovakian group was mainly German, but there were also about a hundred *Volksdeutsche* from Slovakia. The Romanian group had German cadres and about seventy *Volksdeutsche* from Romania. The two companies trained in Korneuburg, a town north-east of Vienna, in espionage, sabotage and the organisation of resistance nests behind enemy lines. From September until April 1945, the Romanian volunteers were parachuted into their homeland in small groups or individually. In December 1944, the *SS-Jagdverband 'Südost'*, whose headquarters were in Zagreb, saw its numbers swell significantly: the two previously mentioned *Einsatzgruppen* were joined by the *Einsatzgruppe 'Serbien-Kroatien'*, the *Einsatzgruppe 'Ungarn'* and the *Einsatzgruppe 'Bulgarien'*, while the *Einsatzgruppe 'Rumänien'* received 175 additional recruits. Most of these units were based in Hollabrunn and Stockerau, north-west of Korneuburg, with the exception of *Einsatzgruppe 'Serbien-Kroatien'*, based in Zagreb.

On the left, a graduate gives the last orders to a squad before an action. On the right, members of a German special unit aboard a boat cross a river.

German soldiers on board a dinghy.

In January 1945, the term *'Einsatzgruppe'* was replaced by the more evocative *'Jagdeinsatz'*. In the course of the same month, a *Jagdeinsatz 'Albanien'* was formed in Zagreb, which reinforced the *Jagdverband*. Amongst the operations launched by the *SS-Jagdverband 'Südost'*, there was also an attempt to supply the besieged in Budapest: on 31 December 1944, the *Jagdkommando 'Donau'*, consisting of thirty men from the *Waffen-SS*, Vlassov's army and the *Kriegsmarine*, left their base in Dunalmaas and, on board boats, sailed up the Danube towards the Hungarian capital. *The commandos wore civilian clothes and were supposed to wear Soviet uniforms* once they crossed enemy lines. But the action failed: the special unit's boats ran aground along the river and had to be abandoned. Soviet patrols discovered them shortly afterwards. Some men managed to escape and reach the German lines via the Pilis Mountains, north-west of Budapest.

The Axis Forces

In March, *SS-Jagdeinsätze 'Serbien-Kroatien'*, *'Albanien'* and *SS-Kommando Kampfschule* left Zagreb to join the rest of the unit in Stockerau. This was engaged against Soviet troops on the Austro-Hungarian border, in the Nickelsdorf sector. The *SS-Jagdverband* fell back via Berendorf, Zöbersdorf and Singerin. In April, the unit fought at St.Pölten, St.Reith and Treisen and then reached Linz. Here, it received orders to reach the 'Alpine Redoubt'. The unit finally surrendered to the Allies in May 1945.

SS-Jagdverband 'Südwest'

In the autumn of 1944, the *SS-Jagdverband 'Südwest'* (under the orders of *SS-Stubaf.* Beck, of the *SS-Hstuf.* Gerlach and later of the *SS-Hstuf.* Traege) was formed from the *Streifkorps 'Südfrankreich'*. In January 1945, it comprised four German and four foreign companies. Later, the companies were reorganised into three *Jagdeinsätze*:

- SS-Jagdeinsatz 'Italien'
- SS-Jagdeinsatz 'Nordfrankreich'
- SS-Jagdeinsatz 'Südfrankreich'

The SS unit operated in the Black Forest, in the Freudenstadt sector, against troops of the *7th US Army*. Its missions mainly involved sabotage, destruction of bridges in particular. The combat school (*Kampfschule*), which had been established in Stuttgart, moved to Ulm in March 1945. The bulk of the *SS-Jagdverband* fell back with *Heeresgruppe 'G'* in the direction of Austria. It is not known whether it managed to reach Linz where Skorzeny and the *SS-Jagdverbände 'Mitte'* and *'Südost'* awaited it.

SS-Fallschirmjäger and Tiger II in Budapest, October 1944.

German half-tracks engaged in combat.

Latvian volunteers of the *SS-Jagdverband 'Ost'*.

Von Fölkersam with Baltic volunteers.

SS-Jagdverband 'Ost'

The *SS-Jagdverband 'Ost'* traces its origin to the *Streifkorps Einsatzgruppe 'Baltikum'* of the Brandenburg *commandos*. The latter had quickly grown from a platoon to a battalion consisting of four companies later reorganised into three *SS-Jagdeinsätze*: *'Russland'*, *'Polen'* and *'Ostland'*. In August 1944, he was ordered to drive the 2,000-strong *Kampfgruppe 'Scherhorn'*, which was wandering through the forests north of Minsk, back towards the German lines. For this operation (codenamed *'Freischütz'*), some 20 men, divided into four groups, were parachuted in near Borissow, Geveny, Dzerschinsk and Witejka. Each of these groups comprised two Germans and three Russians. At the beginning of September, when the Brandenburg *commandos* came under the control of the *Waffen-SS*, the connection with *Kampfgruppe 'Scherhorn'* was established. The *Streifkorps 'Baltikum'* was renamed *SS-Jagdverband 'Ost'*. The *SS-Hstuf.* von Fölkersam then ensured the supply of the surrounded units. In November, Scherhorn divided his group into two marching columns (one of which was commanded by *SS-Oberjunker* Linder, of the *SS-Jagdverband 'Ost'*) and headed north towards Lithuania. The two columns disappeared in the blizzard. Scherhorn, aided by SS commandos, still managed to cover 250 kilometres behind the Soviet lines.

Adrian von Fölkersam in army uniform with the Knight's Cross around his neck.

The Axis Forces

SS-Ostuf. Walter Girg.

The *SS-Jagdverband 'Ost'* also organised an important operation in the Carpathians: it was to block the passes of Jablonika, Borgo, Tulghes, Ghymes and Oltoz in order to slow down the enemy troops and thus prevent the German forces in Greece and Yugoslavia from being cut off from the advance of the Soviets, Bulgarians and Romanians towards Hungary. A hundred men, commanded by *SS-Ustuf.* Walter Girg, were therefore parachuted near the passes, dressed in Romanian, Hungarian and civilian uniforms. The SS men were divided into several groups. The one led by *SS-Ustuf.* Walter Girg managed to divert enemy units from their destination. But he was eventually discovered and captured. The SS soldiers were all executed. The *SS-Ustuf.* Girg miraculously escaped death, while the rest of his comrades were killed. He reached the German lines on foot. For this action, he was decorated with the Knight's Cross. In December 1944, the *SS-Jagdverband 'Ost'* was ordered to liaise with Bandera's Ukrainian nationalists who continued to operate beyond the Soviet lines. This mission (*Unternehmen 'Brauner Bär'*) was assigned to *SS-Hstuf.* Kern and was a success. Kern reached the German lines in April 1945, losing only five men during the operation.

In January 1945, the command of the unit was assigned to *SS-Stubaf.* Adrian von Fölkersam. The unit was now based in Inowroclaw (*Hohensalza* in German), north-east of Poznan (Posen). It was engaged in the defence of the city threatened by two Soviet army corps from 18 January 1945. The situation immediately proved difficult. Encircled, the *SS-Jagdverband 'Ost'* attempted a breakthrough manoeuvre in the night of 21-22 January. Of the eight hundred men who took part in the fighting, only fifteen finally managed to reach Friedenthal a week later. Adrian von Fölkersam was among the many casualties. While the bulk of the *Jagdverband* was being annihilated in Inowroclaw, Walter Girg, promoted to *SS-Obersturmführer* after his action in the Carpathians, was given the mission to carry out a reconnaissance to spot the Soviet armoured vanguards in Pomerania and East Prussia and to identify their targets.

Accompanied by twelve Germans and twelve Russians, Girg reached East Prussia by sea, took possession of two *T-34s* and began a 1,500-kilometre odyssey over the Soviet lines, from Danzig to Kolberg. Here, SS *commandos* joined the besieged, placed under the orders of *SS-Obf.* Heinz Bertling. The latter, mistaking them for renegades, found them guilty of treason and ordered their execution. Fortunately for them, Skorzeny managed to meet Bertling and convinced him that they were his men.

SS-Sturmbannführer SKORZENY

This new action earned Walter Girg promotion to *SS-Hauptsturmführer* and the Oak Fringes for his Knight's Cross.

In April 1945, what remained of the *Jagdverband 'Ost'*, which came under the orders of the *SS-Ostubaf.* Schrage-Bobet, was sent to reinforce the defence of Neustrelitz in the Oderberg-Angermünde sector. The unit was located for the last time at Sachsenhausen/Nordbahn. A company was detached to *Heeresgruppe 'Mitte'*, to destroy a bridge over which Soviet supplies were passing towards the Breslau sector. This mission did not, however, affect the development of operations in Silesia. The company managed to return to the German lines and fought until May in Czechoslovakia where they were annihilated.

SS-Jagdverband 'Nordwest'

The *SS-Jäger-Bataillon 'Nordwest'* was organised in October 1944 from the *Streifkorps 'Nordfrankreich'* of the *Brandenburg* commandos. It comprised 4 companies and then 8, when it was renamed *SS-Jagdverband 'Nordwest'* the following month. There were 4 German companies and 4 companies of Danish, Norwegian, Belgian and Dutch legionnaires. In January 1945, the unit was sent to fight on the Oder front, on the Schwedt bridgehead. It defended the Niepperwiese sector from 1 February to 3 March. Later placed in the reserve of the *3.Panzerarmee*, the unit disappeared during the offensive launched on 16 April by the Soviets. Its commanders had been *SS-Hstuf.* Hoyer and later Dethier.

SS-Jagdverband 'Süd'

Unit of which only the name of its commander is known, the *SS-Stubaf.* Dr Otto Begus. It is not mentioned in the order of battle of 4 October 1944.

Notes

[1] SS-FHA, Amt II Org.Abt.Ia/II Tgb.Nr.3473/44 g.Kdos

[2] A plateau located between Wallonia, Belgium and the German states of Rhineland-Palatinate and North Rhine-Westphalia.

Bibliography

Charles Trang, "*Dictionnaire de la Waffen-SS, vol. IV*", Edizioni Heimdal
Massimiliano Afiero, "*Waffen-SS in guerra, volume IV: battaglie e campagne dimenticate*", Associazione Culturale Ritterkreuz
Jean-Paul Pallud, "*Ardennes 1944 Peiper & Skorzeny*", Serie Elite, Osprey Pyblishing
Craig W. H. Luther, Hugh Page Taylor, "*For Germany: the Otto Skorzeny memoirs*", Bender Publishing

Waffen-Hauptsturmführer Miervaldis Adamsons

by Cesare Veronesi

Miervaldis Adamsons, first right, wearing the uniform of the Latvian National Army.

Members of a Latvian police battalion, during an anti-partisan operation, March 1943.

Miervaldis Adamsons was born on 29 June 1910 in Poltava, Russia, to a family of Latvian origin. In 1920, his family decided to return to Latvia and moved to Cēsis, where Miervaldis graduated from the local grammar school. In 1928, Miervaldis began his studies in theology at the University of Riga. During this time, he became a member of the oldest Latvian student fraternity, called *'Latvia'*. In 1929, however, he left his studies to join the Merchant Navy. During his travels he visited Africa and South America, but due to his gloomy character and his inclination to always get into trouble, after a disagreement with the ship's captain, he disembarked in 1930 in Marseilles, France. There he enlisted in the Foreign Legion, signing a six-year contract. He served in Morocco in the cavalry units and was decorated several times for his bravery, which earned him the nickname *'Moroccan Terror'* and promotion to non-commissioned officer. After his service in the Foreign Legion ended, he returned to Latvia and in 1937, enlisted in the Latvian army, serving as an officer in the 8th Infantry Regiment *'Daugavpils'*.

At war

Following the Soviet occupation of the country in 1940, the Latvian army was disbanded. Like many of his compatriots, Ādamsons hid in the forests of his region to escape capture and deportation. When German forces invaded Latvia in the summer of 1941, Ādamsons led an anti-communist partisan unit in the Vidzeme region, which was immediately involved in fighting against retreating Soviet units. Immediately afterwards, he volunteered in the *Lettische Polizei Front Bataillon 26 Tukums*, deployed from June 1942 in the Minsk region and engaged against Soviet partisan formations. In February 1943, Ādamsons while leading a patrol on the frozen surface of Lake Ilmen, between Soviet lines, managed to destroy an enemy ammunition depot and capture a Soviet officer.

Defensive position of the Latvian SS Brigade, with an *MG-34* on a tripod, on the Leningrad front, spring 1943.

Latvian volunteers on a defensive position.

On 26 March 1943, he was decorated with the Iron Cross Second Class. In April 1943, Ādamsons served in the *2nd Bataillon* of the Latvian Brigade on the Leningrad Front, engaged on the Volchov Front. During heavy fighting, he was severely wounded in the head and one eye. On 15 September 1943, he was decorated with the Black Wounded Badge and on 21 September 1943, with the Iron Cross First Class.

The Knight's Cross

After a period of convalescence, he was placed in command of the *6.Kp./Waffen-Grenadier-Regiment der SS 44* of the *19. Waffen-Grenadier-Division der SS (lettische Nr.2)*, formed with

The Axis Forces

Waffen-Ostuf. Miervaldis Adamsons, summer 1944.

An assault cannon in winter livery, 1944.

the elements of the Latvian SS Brigade. He was again wounded in combat in August 1944, shortly before being promoted to the rank of *Hauptsturmführer* in September 1944. Also in the summer of 1944, on 25 August 1944 to be precise, he was decorated with the Bronze Badge for hand-to-hand combat. Returning to the front, he took part with his unit in the fighting in the Curlandia pocket in December 1944, again being severely wounded, complaining of partial loss of sight. His company repelled no less than seven Soviet attacks in a single day, and at the end of the battle, the bodies of four hundred Soviet soldiers lay in front of the Latvian positions. The fighting was fierce and entire Soviet units were annihilated. For valour shown in battle, Adamsons was decorated with the Knight's Cross on 25 January 1945. We read the proposal for the award of the *Ritterkreuz*, written on 2 January 1945, by *SS-Gruf.* Bruno Streckenbach, commander of the *19.SS*:

"*...On 29.12.1944, the 6th company of the* Waffen-Gren.Rgt. d.SS-44 (Lett. No. 6), *was in the Vanagi sector under the command of* Waffen-Hstuf. *Adamsons and in the fighting that took place in the same sector, it distinguished itself for its valour. After hours of drumming fire, the enemy soldiers, with the strength of two regiments, regrouped and went on the attack to take the important foothold in Vanagi. Over the next thirty-six hours, the enemy brought thirteen attacks that were repulsed, after inflicting heavy casualties. In the afternoon, with five* Sturmgeschütze *and about two hundred men under the* *command of the* Waffen-Hstuf. *Adamsons a counter-attack was launched. The core of the resistance at the Vanagi support point was the* Waffen-Hstuf. *Adamsons, who at this juncture was wounded for the second time in combat. He remained on his position, however, and continued to urge his men to fight. The* Sturmgeschütze *thus returned forward, with their gallant crews, to come to the aid of the support point. Once they reached the position, they reported that no more reinforcements would arrive and that the men would have to endure the hail of enemy artillery shells and cannons. Numerous acts of heroism and valiant deeds were performed here by only a few men against a far superior enemy.*

Defensive position in Courland with a mortar.

Latvian defensive position on the Courland front.

Thanks to his determination and iron will, the company commander, the Waffen-Hstuf. *Adamsons spurred the men on to complete a superhuman task. The loss of the important foothold, which was the basis for all future defensive fighting, would have allowed the enemy to penetrate between our lines and would have forced us to make a considerable retreat of the front line. This threat was foiled. In front of the Vanagi support point, a Russian infantry force equal to a division was destroyed, precluding these men from being engaged in combat again...'.*

The Axis Forces

Adamsons with his wife Catherine.

The proposal was also supported by SS-Ogruf. Walter Krüger, commander of the VI. SS-Frw. Armee-Korps: *"...On his own initiative, [Adamsons] went to the front to support the attack although enemy units had already penetrated on both sides of our defensive array. Particularly noteworthy is that this Latvian officer was wounded five times in combat. I particularly support the proposal to award the Knight's Cross to this brave Latvian officer'*.

The end of the war and imprisonment

In the spring of 1945, Ādamsons was admitted to various military hospitals in Courland. During the last days during the fighting in the Curlandia pocket, some of his comrades offered him a place on a boat to escape to Sweden, as many Latvian soldiers and civilians were doing, but Adamsons refused to leave Latvia. In May 1945, while still in hospital, he was captured by the Soviets. After declaring that he was a German soldier, he was sent to a prison camp in Šiauliai and then worked as a 'forced' labourer in the nickel mines in Murmansk. After a few months, he and other German officers attempted to escape to Finland during the winter of 1945/1946. However, he was caught near the Finnish border. In May 1946, after his Latvian nationality was established, he was sentenced to death as a traitor. Miervaldis Adamsons was shot in Riga on 23 August 1946. In 1993, Adamsons was completely exonerated of all charges by the Latvian Supreme Court.

Decorations
Iron Cross Second Class: 26 March 1943
Black Wounded Badge: 15 September 1943
Iron Cross First Class: 21 September 1943
Silver Wounded Badge: 12 April 1944
Brooch for hand-to-hand combat: 25 August 1944
Gold Wounded Badge: 1 September 1944
Infantry Assault Badge: 14 October 1944
Knight's Cross: 25 January 1945.

Bibliography
Veit Scherzer, "*Die Ritterkreuzträger 1939–1945*"
Arthur Silgailis, "*Latvian Legion*", J. Bender Publishing
Hans Stober, "*Die lettischen divisionen im VI SS-Armeekorps*"

"Only the strong took to the field, to the shame of their brothers"
1st Assault Legion 'Tagliamento' 1943 - 1945
by Paolo Crippa

The labarum of the LXIII *Tagliamento* Legion of the MVSN, from which the 1st M Assault Legion *Tagliamento* originated after 8 September 1943.

Two Blackshirts of the *Tagliamento* of the Italian Social Republic (*Pisanò*).

In the summer of 1941, the LXIII M Battalion *'Tagliamento'* of the Milizia Volontaria Sicurezza Nazionale (Volunteer National Security Militia) was sent to the Soviet Union, as part of the 3rd *'Celere'* Division, to take part in the Italian-German offensive. After fighting on the Dnjeper, in January 1943, he was involved in the massive Soviet offensive and was swept away with the entire A.R.M.I.R. during Operation *'Saturn'*, being decimated in personnel. Back in Italy, the Battalion was reconstituted and included in the newly formed 1st Legionary Armoured Division 'M' in the summer of the same year. After Mussolini's arrest on 25 July, the Division, which came under the control of the Royal Army and was placed in a de facto 'waiting state', changed its name to 136th Armoured Division *'Centauro II'*. The Armistice saw the Division away from the fighting that followed those hot days and, after a few days, the Germans took back the armaments they had ceded to the Italian unit, without a blow. In those convulsive days, the LXIII M Battalion, composed mostly of men from central Italy and the north-eastern regions, abandoned the *'Centauro'* Division and joined the Officer's Cadet Battalion in Ostia and the XVI 'M' Battalion, forming the nucleus of what was to become the *'Tagliamento Legion'*. The Legionnaires became part of the German 2nd Parachute Division and, for this reason, had to take the German military oath. With the constitution of the Italian Social Republic (23 September 1943), the unit assumed the name of 1st Assault Division M "*Tagliamento*", later framed in the Republican National

Flag of the 1st M Assault Legion *Tagliamento* (*Pisanò*).

Guard, commanded by First Senior (later Lieutenant Colonel) Merìco Zuccàri. From that moment on, the Tagliamento Legion was trained and armed with the precise aim of carrying out anti-partisan operations and was deployed in the Apennine mountains in operations to round up former Anglo-American prisoners who had escaped from concentration camps. The original *'Tagliamento'* was disbanded on 23 November and, until 30 November, the LXIII Battalion remained in Ardea, for counter-guerrilla training. On that date, due to the good evidence provided before the Armistice, the G.N.R. General Command authorised the reconstitution of the *'Tagliamento'* Legion, which was sent to the province of Brescia. Here, it was based in Chiari from where, on the morning of 10 December, the 1st Company left to carry out a raid on Mount *Darfo*, where a strong group of well-armed partisans was being organised. The partisans' reaction was strong, two soldiers were killed and the company commander wounded, but the partisan nucleus was practically annihilated. On 19 December 1943, the order to move to the Vercellese area arrived, as the situation was worsening, especially in Valsesia. The Battalion therefore moved from Chiari to Vercelli, where it was quartered in the "*Conte di Torino*" barracks, immediately renamed "*Tagliamento*". The following day, the Battalion moved to Borgosesia, in the centre of the area where Moscatelli's partisans had begun their activities and had managed to eliminate a good part of the Carabinieri from the local station.

The Legion implemented a particularly violent repressive policy: proclamations were issued, threatening the execution of ten hostages for every republican or German soldier killed. The threat was first implemented in Borgosesia on 22 December, following the previous day's killing of two Legion soldiers.

On the evening of Christmas Eve 1943, the 1st Company went to garrison the village of Crocemosso Santa Maria, setting up positions on the mountains of Vallemosso, which were immediately targeted by partisan attacks. On 31 December, the Legion unleashed a combing operation, going up Valsesia in force, clashing several times with the partisans of commander Moscatelli and suffering serious losses. The anti-guerrilla operations in

Valsesia continued throughout the month of January, with the aim of 'clearing' the entire valley of partisan units, deploying all available forces and even using an armed train. At the end of January 1944, the 'Camilluccia' Battalion arrived from Rome, made up exclusively of volunteers, which became the 2nd Battalion of the Legion.

L3/38 tank of the 'Tagliamento' in Valsesia in the spring of 1944. The Legion had three of these small tanks until the departure for Marche (Borgatti).

Group photo of a unit of the 'Tagliamento' Legion at the end of a round-up in Valsesia in April 1944. Many militiamen are armed with Sten machine guns, captured from allied airplanes destined for the partisans (Pisanò).

In Valsesia, the civil war showed its cruellest side and the clashes with the partisans continued unabated throughout the spring: the legionaries of the 'Tagliamento' found themselves facing ambushes, attacks on garrisons, ambushes, responding with sometimes bloody reprisals, which also ended with the killing of civilians and the burning of houses. The legion remained in the Vercellese-Biellese area until the end of May 1944 and at the end of the month came the order for a new transfer, this time to the Marches, in the Tuscan-Marchigiano

Apennines: on 4 June 1944, after parading in front of G.N.R. Commander Renato Ricci, the '*Tagliamento*' left for the new area of operations.

Legionaries of the 'Tagliamento' parade through the streets of Vercelli.

The pennant of the 1st Battalion of the '*Tagliamento*' Legion with the motto '*Follow me!*' in Vercelli in June 1944 (*Pisanò*).

The Command moved to Sasso Corvaro (PU), the Pesaro area, to assist the German deployment on that stretch of the Gothic Line. The Battalions provided security for the Pioneers of the Engineer Corps, intent on building the 'Green Line', which was to be a part of the Gothic Line, operating between the province of Arezzo and Pesaro. In this circumstance, friction emerged with the German Commands in the conduct of anti-partisan repression and also with the forced labour organisations (Todt and the Paladino Organisation) in the search for republican draft dodgers. It was, however, a period of relative calm compared to the very tense period in Valsesia. At the end of August, when the retreating German units were beginning to establish themselves on the

'*Green Line*', the '*Tagliamento*' Legion was transferred to the Vicenza area, occupying the towns of Torrebelvicino, Staro, Recoaro Terme and San Vito di Leguzzano.

Legion soldiers returning from an action on board FIAT 666 trucks, probably in Valsesia (*Crippa*).

Father Antonio Intreccialagli, chaplain of the '*Tagliamento*'.

The "*Tagliamento*" participated as a mobile unit, alongside Ukrainian units, in all the combing operations in the province of Vicenza, on the Schio Plain, in Thiene, on the Asiago Plateau and on Mount Ortigara. On 10 August, the Legion's units were dislocated as follows: the LXIII Battalion Headquarters in Recoaro, the 3rd Company in Staro, the 1st Battalion "*Camilluccia*" Headquarters and the 4th Company in Valli di Pasubio, the 5th Company in San Vito di Leguzzano. The U.P.I. (Ufficio Politico Investigativo) was stationed at Torrebelvicino, which unfortunately soon became infamous for the atrocious tortures to which it subjected not only partisans captured with weapons, but any person who, along a chain of denunciations, was suspected of being a danger to the formation. Colonel Zuccari issued a communiqué stating: '*The U.P.I. is under the direct and exclusive command of the Legion Commander, who is its leader*'. From there, in September 1944, the '*Tagliamento*' took to the upper Treviso area, on the border with the upper Vicenza area, where towards the end of the month the fiercest and most prolonged

The Axis Forces

Young mascots of the Legion (*Pisanò*).

anti-Partisan repression in the area of Monte Grappa, which claimed almost 500 lives. In Bassano there was a cruel demonstration action: on 26 September, 31 rebels were hanged from the trees of the city's northern ramparts and their corpses were left exposed for four days. On 28 October, the Legion moved to Alta Val Camonica, deploying garrisons in Ponte di Legno, Temù, Vione, Vezza d'Oglio, Monno, Carteno and Malonno. After carrying out operations in the Upper Valley, on 5 November, the entire Legion began to move southwards, to garrison the entrance to Val Camonica, to protect important fortification works: the Command moved to Pisogne, the 1st Battalion between Dario and Marone (with a Company in Zone) and the 2nd Battalion to the entrance of Val Borlezza. Starting in November, the Legion took part in counter-guerrilla actions, in concert with the garrisons of the local Black Brigades.

Officers of the 'Tagliamento' and their German counterparts during a demonstration (*Pisanò*).

However, after the Alexander Proclamation, the partisan formations had temporarily almost completely ceased all activity and therefore the '*Tagliamento*' was particularly engaged in police operations, aimed at flushing out draft dodgers and political agitators . At the end of the year, the '*Tagliamento*' Command issued a summary report of the operations in Valcamonica:

Another photo taken on the same occasion: in the centre, Colonel Merico Zuccari, commander of the '*Tagliamento*'.

Militia of the '*Tagliamento*' departing for an action (*Crippa*).

A unit of the '*Tagliamento*' on the march, 1944.

Casualties suffered: fallen: 2 officers, 3 non-commissioned officers, 44 legionnaires; wounded: 8 officers, 12 non-commissioned officers, 83 legionnaires.

Losses inflicted: 750 enemy prisoners captured; 431 bandits killed; 401 bandits captured; 136 facilitators arrested; 338 renegades and deserters captured.

Captured Weapons and Material: 1 47/32 cannon; 1 81 mm mortar; 8 machine guns of various models; 17 Italian and foreign machine guns; 275 Model '91 and *Mauser* muskets; 114 automatic muskets; 19,000 cartridges for small arms; 1,033 hand grenades; 7 quintals of explosives; 10 mines. With the arrival of the spring of 1945, the partisan bands reconstituted themselves, also armed by numerous allied drops. The German Command decided that the Mortirolo was the point to attack, because it was a strategic area, which connected the upper Valcamonica with the Valtellina and had for some time become a safe hiding place for American soldiers who had fled captivity, deserters from the Salò army and partisans of the Green Flames, who were concentrating their units there. At the beginning of February 1945, General of the SS,

Mussolini visited the units of the 'Tagliamento' in the Marches on 6 August 1944 (*Arena*).

The Duce talks with a young legionnaire (*Pisanò Archive*).

Karl Heinz Bürger, commander of the German police in northern Italy - East (Veneto and eastern Lombardy) assigned the task of attacking the Mortirolo Pass to the *'Tagliamento'* Legion. The German Command did not reveal that this move, in addition to the reasons outlined above, concealed the intention of the German forces to take full control of State Road 42 of Tonale and Mendola, in order to ensure an escape route for the German troops towards Trentino, in case State Road 12 of the Brenner Pass proved impassable, in view of a possible retreat. On 22 February, the offensive was launched and Zuccaro's troops, with the support of a few German soldiers from an artillery section, were convinced they could carry out a rapid annihilation action.

In fact, the partisans, having been warned of the preparations, were able to organise themselves and also find a small country gun. The attackers were therefore blocked by a heavy barrage and retreated, remaining clumsy in the snow; the winter uniforms of the "*Tagliamento*" militia were also made of dark cloth and this allowed the partisans to target them accurately. The next day, the fascists returned to the attack, managing to get close to the positions of the Green Flames, but, unable to break through, they had to fall back again, leaving the bodies of dead comrades and numerous weapons and ammunition on the field. The fighting continued until day 27, without the *'Tagliamento'* being able to reach and occupy the positions held by the Green Flames. According to data provided by Legion veterans, as many as 45 per cent of the attacking forces were killed or wounded. This raised the morale of the partisans, who went on the attack and on 28 February unsuccessfully attacked the Viezza D'Olio barracks. For the entire month of March, the "*Tagliamento*" Legionnaires, with low morale, limited themselves to garrisoning the territory, intercepting a few Allied air raids. This convinced the Legion Command that the partisans might be running out of weapons and ammunition, because supplies had been captured by the "*Tagliamento*" and so the decision was taken to launch a new attack on the Mortirolo Pass.

The Axis Forces

A legionnaire, armed with a British STEN machine gun taken from the partisans, stands guard in front of a garrison of the *'Tagliamento'* (Pisanò).

On the morning of 9 April, Colonel Zuccari ordered the start of the so-called *'Mughetto Action'*: the LXIII Battalion 'M' began to move up the valley, to bring new attacks on the partisan forces barricaded on the mountain. The action was also supported by 300 men of the 2nd Battalion of the Italian *Waffen SS* of the 82nd Grenadier Regiment, under the command of Major Sergio Bianchi, from Como, and two Companies of the 5th Mobile Black Alpine Brigade *'Enrico Quagliata'*, commanded by Lieutenant Colonel Arturo Pellegrini. Despite several attacks, none of them succeeded in breaking through the partisan lines: the predominant position of the Green Flames, who were entrenched in a system of trenches and fortifications on the top of the Mortirolo mountain dating back to the Great War, proved crucial to the victory. The toughest battle took place on 19 April: at 6:00 a.m. German howitzers began to bombard the top of the pass from the bottom of the valley, concentrating on a farmstead where the partisan command was believed to be located, and the bombardment ended at around midday. This was followed by a coordinated attack between the forces of the *'Tagliamento'* and some *Wehrmacht* divisions, which were trying to retreat from the Val Camonica. The courage and excellent behaviour of the attackers were to no avail, as the positions were situated too high; come evening, the "*Tagliamento*" fell back, forced to mercifully leave the wounded in the field. On 25 April, the national insurrection was unleashed and General Cadorna, commander-in-chief of the "Corpo Volontari della Libertà", issued an ultimatum to the R.S.I. troops, which was also sent, via a parish priest, to the "*Tagliamento*" Command.

To this missive, the Legion Commander replied on 27 April, through the parish priest of Mouno: *'The Camonica Valley is now destined to become a battlefield. The German troops are not surrendering. If the 'Green Flames' do not carry out acts of hostility against the 'Tagliamento', this unit will not act against the 'Green Flames' themselves. At every act of hostility on the part of the 'Green Flames' it will be the villages of the valley that will suffer reprisals'.*

The Partisan Command replied to Colonel Zuccaro in these terms: *'We have received your negative reply to our intimation of surrender. Intimation made in the name of the National Liberation Committee for Upper Italy. We had believed that we were speaking as Italian soldiers to an Italian soldier, from whom we were divided by differences in ideals and political conceptions,*

Another photo of Father Intreccialagli in action. The priest, armed with a MAB, wears a camouflage shirt made from Italian M1929 fabric.

but to whom we were still to unite the bonds of having all belonged to the same Army that had once fought the same enemies of our Homeland. We were wrong. You, Mr Merico Zuccari, are no longer a soldier or even an Italian, you are a vulgar and bloodthirsty leader in the pay of Italy's enemies. You try to defend your German masters, to threaten and carry out reprisals against innocent people. No soldier of the 'Tagliamento' will escape the punishment that awaits him. We give you one word, and be assured that we will keep it: we 'Green Flames' of the 'Tito Speri' will execute you all. Commander Sandro'. In the following days, the assaults continued, but they did not create any problems for the partisans, because they were carried out for the most part by retreating stragglers, who did not agree to surrender. The Command gave the order that the units of the "Tagliamento" were to head towards Tonale, from where they were to head towards Trentino; the SS Italian Battalion decided instead to converge on Tirano. From Edolo, after a one-day halt, the Legion reached Monno. From there, on 29 April, the "Tagliamento", together with aliquots of the 5th Mobile Black Alpine Brigade and elements of the Territorial GNR Garrisons, began the march along State Road 42, in the direction of the Tonale Pass. On 2 May, the last shots were fired, while the units of the 1st Assault Legion "M" "Tagliamento" continued into Trentino, where they surrendered to the C.L.N. in Revò and Fondo, Trentino, on 5 May. Three isolated garrisons that had not managed to reach the bulk of the Legion were attacked by partisans and the soldiers, for the most part, killed as promised by Commandant Sandro. On the night of 27-28 April 1945, 43 young militiamen of the 1st Assault Legion 'Tagliamento' were summarily killed in Rovetta. These young men were garrisoned at the Presolana Cantoniera, commanded by Second Lieutenant Roberto Panzanelli, and had set off armed along the valley, preceded by a white flag carried by Alessandro Franceschetti, the hotelier where the militiamen were staying. When they reached Rovetta, they decided to lay down their weapons and give themselves up to the local National Liberation Committee. However, Lieutenant Panzelli was unaware that this self-proclaimed C.L.N. had no real powers and therefore the promised guarantees were worthless. On 28 April, a group of partisans from the 53rd Garibaldi Brigade 'Thirteen Martyrs', the 'Camozzi' Brigade and the Green Flames arrived in the village. They took the soldiers from the school where they were being held and brought them to the village cemetery. Sub-lieutenant Panzanelli tried in vain to enforce the paper in his possession with the signed guarantees, but the paper with the signatures was snatched from his hand and trampled on. When they reached the cemetery, two firing squads were organised and 43 of the prisoners, aged between 15 and 22, were shot. Only three of them were spared because of their young age; Legionnaire Fernando Caciolo, who had managed to escape during the transfer march to the cemetery in Rovetta, finding refuge in the house of a priest, also escaped the sad fate.

Organigram
- Command Company
- I (formerly LXIII) Battalion M '*Tagliamento*'
  o Command
  o Command Platoon
  o 1st Company
  o 2nd Company
  o 3rd Company
- II Battalion M '*Camilluccia*'
  o Command
  o Command Platoon
  o 4th Company
  o 5th Company
  o 6th Company
- Autoreparto
- Accompanying Weapons Company

Armament
The 'Tagliamento' Legion had sufficient weapons to cover its needs: '91 muskets, M.A.B., STEN captured from partisans, Breda 30 machine guns, MG-42 heavy machine guns, 45mm Brixia mortars, 81mm mortars and three German PAK 37 anti-tank guns.

Vehicles
The 'Tagliamento' had a discrete fleet of vehicles: 6 Fross - Bussing trucks, 12 Ford trucks, 2 cars and 2 motorbikes. From some period pictures and according to the testimonies of some veterans, the Legion also had at least 2 FIAT 666 trucks with trailers.

Losses
During the approximately two years of the Legion's life, the 'Tagliamento' claimed 237 dead and over 300 wounded.

Bibliography
Arena Nino, "*R.S.I. – Forze Armate della Repubblica Sociale – La guerra in Italia – 1943 – 1944 – 1945*", Ermanno Albertelli Editore.
Crippa Paolo, "*I Reparti Corazzati della Repubblica Sociale Italiana 1943 -1945*", Marvia Edizioni.
Crippa Paolo, "*I mezzi corazzati italiani della guerra civile 1943-1945*", Mattioli 1885
Cucut Carlo, "*Le Forze Armate della R.S.I. 1943 – 1945 – Forze di terra*", G.M.T., Trento, 2005.
Malatesta Leonardo, "*La Legione Tagliamento dal 1923 al 1945. La nascita, il suo impiego bellico nella Seconda guerra mondiale e la guerra civile*", Centro Studi e Ricerche Storiche "*Silentes Loquimur*", Pordenone, 2012.

The 162. (Turk.) Infanterie-Division
by Danilo Morisco
Military-historical consulting by Pierluigi Romeo di Colloredo Mels

Members of the Turkestan Legion, spring 1943.

Turkestani volunteers engaged on the front line, 1942.

Turkestani volunteers in the German army, 1943.

In the first months of Operation *Barbarossa*, the Germans had to cope with a huge influx of prisoners of war, it seems up to 5.7 million men, mostly Muslims. Of these, some three million died in the camps or from disease, in addition to those who were killed purely for racial reasons. Those with 'Mediterranean' or 'Mongolian' features, regarded as 'carriers of Bolshevism', were particularly hard hit at the beginning of the occupation. It seems that only 6% of the Turkmen prisoners survived their imprisonment in the second half of 1941. However, between October and November of that year, the first Turkmen and Caucasian volunteer units were formed, consisting mainly of former prisoners. In addition to covering the heavy losses suffered by the *Wehrmacht* on the Eastern Front, the prisoner soldiers, especially Turkestans, could have furthered Hitler's intention to bring Turkey into the war on the side of Germany. Besides this, several national committees were formed in Berlin, mainly by emigrants from Russian Turkestan and western Russia (Ukraine and Crimea), whose main tasks were to provide propaganda and intelligence activities. In the Turkestan National Unity Committee (Millî *Türkistan Birligi Komitesi*) for example, out of twelve sections, five were in charge of propaganda (magazines, newspapers, radio). Already by the beginning of 1942, 53,000 Cossacks (*Kosaken-Kavallerie-Korps*), 310,000 Russians, 250,000 Ukrainians, 5,000 Kalmyks, 180,000 Turkestans, 110,000 Caucasians, 40,000 Volga Tatars and 20,000 Crimean Tatars had joined the German Forces, making a total of 968,000 men.

Russia, 1943: German senior officers, with General Hellmich in the middle, during an inspection of an infantry battalion of the Turkestan Legion.

In February 1942, in order to organically co-ordinate the Caucasian and Turkish-Tatar volunteer formations that were being formed, the Eastern Legion Staff *(Ostlegionen)* was formed, six legions consisting of several *Ostbatallionen* (Eastern Battalions): the *Turkestanische Legion*, which also included volunteers from other ethnic groups (26 battalions); the *Aserbeidschanische Legion* (14), which included the *II./Sonderverband Bergmann*, the *SS-Waffengruppe Aserbeidschan*, the *Waffengruppe Aserbeidschan* and the *II./Feiwilligen-Stamm Regiment*; the *Nordkaukasische* Legion (9 battalions), consisting of legionnaires from about 30 ethnic groups; the *Wolgatatarische Legion* (7/8) consisting of Bashkiri, Ciuvasci, Udmurti, Mari and Mordvini; *the Kaukasischer Mohammedaner-Legion* (8), formed by Azeris, Dagestanians, Chechens, Ingush and Lezghini; finally, both made up of Christian elements, the *Georgische Legion* (12) and the *Armenische Legion* (12).

Like most of the *Ostlegionen*, however, the commanding officers were predominantly German and, although sources differ on this, it appears that only 87 of the approximately 180,000 Turkestani volunteers were officers and 23 of these, were part of the national committee.

Also at the beginning of 1942, a Turkish-Tatar regiment was formed at *Sicherungsdivision* 444, which would later go into action between the mouth of the Dnieper and the Crimea as *Türk-Batallion* 444.

Another group of Red Army soldiers from Central Asia, after passing to the Germans, formed the unit that in 1942, would become the 450th *Infanteriebataillon*, formed in Legionovo (Poland), specialised in anti-partisan warfare. In May 1943, the *Oberkommando des Heeres* decided to unite the

A Mullah, a Muslim man from the Turkestan Legion.

Ostlegionen[1] into one unit. The troop personnel came from the following units: *Armenische Legion*, *Aserbaidschanische Legion*, *Georgische Legion*, *Nordkaukasische Legion*, *Turkestanische Legion* and *Wolgatatarische Legion*.

Turkestani volunteers during training on the Eastern Front, 1943.

The *Turkestanische Legion* was mobilised in May 1942 and originally consisted of one battalion, in 1943 of 15 and finally, at the end of 1944, of 26, thus mainly integrated as independent battalions into the German divisions.

Parade of wards of an infantry battalion of the Turkestan Legion, 1943.

The 162. (*Turk.*) *Infanterie-Division*

Turkestani volunteers with an anti-tank piece.

Turkestani volunteers, carrying the Legion flag.

On 21 March 1943, the new division was formed in Neuhammer, Silesia (today Świętoszów, Poland), in the *Generalgouvernement*, from the *Stab* of the dissolved 162 *Infanterie-Division*, until then employed as the *Führungsstab* of the *Turkestanische Legion, Aserbaidschanische Legion* and *Georgische Legion*. The commands were formed by the officers of the old 162nd, destroyed by the Soviets at Kalinin in January 1942. *(Turkmenische) Infanterie-Division*, after the old *162. Infanterie-Division*, which had fought on the eastern front during 1941, had been disbanded after suffering enormous losses; the officers and non-commissioned officers belonging to the 'old' *162*.

The Axis Forces

General Oskar Ritter von Niedermayer.

Turkestani volunteers train with a mortar.

The command of the new *162.* was entrusted to General Oskar Ritter von Niedermayer, a profound connoisseur of the Turkish mentality and language. Niedermayer was considered by many historians to be a kind of German Lawrence of Arabia: in 1912, he had led an exploratory trip to Persia and, between 1915 and 1916, together with the orientalist Otto von Hentig (1886-1984), he carried out a mission to Afghanistan to convince the Emir Habibullah Khan (r. 1901-1919) to side with the Central Empires, in view of the emir's sympathies for the Ottoman Empire and Panislamism, and thus start an anti-British revolt in India. Later, having failed this objective, he was ordered to leave Afghanistan for Turkey in mid-1916, where together with other German officers, such as Liman von Sanders, he served as liaison officer and advisor to the Ottoman General Staff. With the opening of the Eastern Front in 1941, General Niedermayer once again became useful to the German Armed Forces: the OKW saw fit to use his knowledge of the Turkish people to organise *Ostlegionen* and he was eventually given command of the *162. Turkmenische-Division*. On 21 March 1943, the division was officially formed in Poland; officers from the original *162.* Division began the training of the unit, after General Niedermayer had taken the decision to train the Caucasian troops from scratch, judging the initial level of preparation of the volunteers to be totally inadequate: the German officer complained above all about the poor discipline of the troops. At the end of May 1943, the new unit was transferred to Neuhammer, where it continued its training period. *The 162.* had Imams who acted as military 'chaplains', in charge of spreading political messages and legitimising the anti-Bolshevik cause. The Legion's flag itself was inspired by the red and blue flag of the Autonomous Republic of Kokand in 1920, with a bow and arrow in the centre.

The Axis Forces

A group of Turkestani volunteers during a training session, 1943.

Turkestan Volunteer, 1943.

Attempts were also made to use Central Asian Common Turkish (Turkî or Chagataic), of which von Niedermayer was a profound connoisseur, as a language of communication, along with German. The division was thus organised:

Infanterie-Regiment 303 (Oberstleutnant Christiani)
Infanterie-Regiment 314 (Oberstleutnant Pohle)
Infanterie-Regiment 329 (from 15/08/1944)
Divisions-Bataillon 162 (Major Kaminsky)
Artillerie-Regiment 236 (Oberstleutnant von le Fort)
Pioneer-Bataillon 936 (Hauptmann Weidlich)
Panzerjäger-Abteilung 236 (Hauptmann Kiesler)
Aufklärungs-Abteilung 236 (Rittmeister Meyer)
Infanterie-Divisions-Nachrichten-Abteilung   236 (Hauptmann Neuber)
Nachschubtruppen 936

OZAK Front

Having completed its training, keeping to the policy of not deploying volunteers from the Red Army on the Eastern Front, the division was initially sent to Slovenia, where it awaited orders for a few weeks. Then, towards the end of August, in view of of the occupation of Italy following the fall of the Mussolini government, it was transferred to northern Italy (*Oberitalien*), reporting to the *II. SS- Panzer-Korps*, which in turn was at the disposal of *Heeresgruppe* B (HG B).

The Axis Forces

Sergeant of the *Turkestanische Legion*. Note the oval shield with the inscription 'BIZ ALLA BILEN', translatable to *'God is with Us'*, introduced since 1942.

The sign of *162.(Turk.) Inf.-Division*.

The Turkestani units were then transferred to the Udine area, where they were temporarily re-equipped with Italian war materiel and weapons. On 29 September, the *II.SS-Pz.Korps* assigned to the *162.(turk.)Inf.Div.* the security zone between the Tagliamento and the Monfalcone-Vipacco-Zolla-Idria-Ziri line. At the same time, all forces in the area of responsibility, including units of the *SS-Karstwehr-Btl.* and the *2.Kroatische Legion*, were subordinated to the division. Starting on 5 October, elements of the *162.(Turk.)Inf.Div.*, in particular *Oberstleuntant* Pohle's *Inf.Rgt.314*, were engaged in the anti-partisan operation *'Felix'*, which was conducted in the Natisone valley from Cividale to Tiglio. The Turkestani units were engaged mainly to be trained in counter-guerrilla tactics and the balance was positive, with 88 partisans killed and 78 prisoners.

From 6 October, in view of a new large-scale round-up operation (Operation *Wolkenbruch*), most of the units of the *162.(turk.)Inf.Div.* were transferred to the area east of Ljubljana and west of Zagreb. The elements that remained in the Udine area formed the *Sicherungsgruppe von le Fort*, under the orders of the commander of *Art.Rgt.236*, *Oberst* Baron von le Fort. The tasks of the security group mainly concerned the protection of the Udine-Tarvisio and Gorizia-Piedicolle railway lines. Operation *Wolkenbruch* officially began on 21 October and ended on 11 November 1943, divided into four main phases. The aim was to eliminate the communist partisan forces in the area between Slovenia and Croatia. The *162.(turk.)Inf.Div.*, with headquarters in Rajhenburg, north of Brestanica, was deployed at the beginning of the operation on the *Reich* border line from the Mirna river to Kostanjevica-Samobor-Karlovac. The operation was successful, the newly formed partisan brigades suffered heavy losses and many had to be disbanded. However, the rapid transfer of the German divisions to other fronts once again left large areas to the partisans, so new operations had to be carried out to maintain control of territory. From 15 November, the divisions engaged in Slovenia were transferred back to Friuli and the Gorizia region.

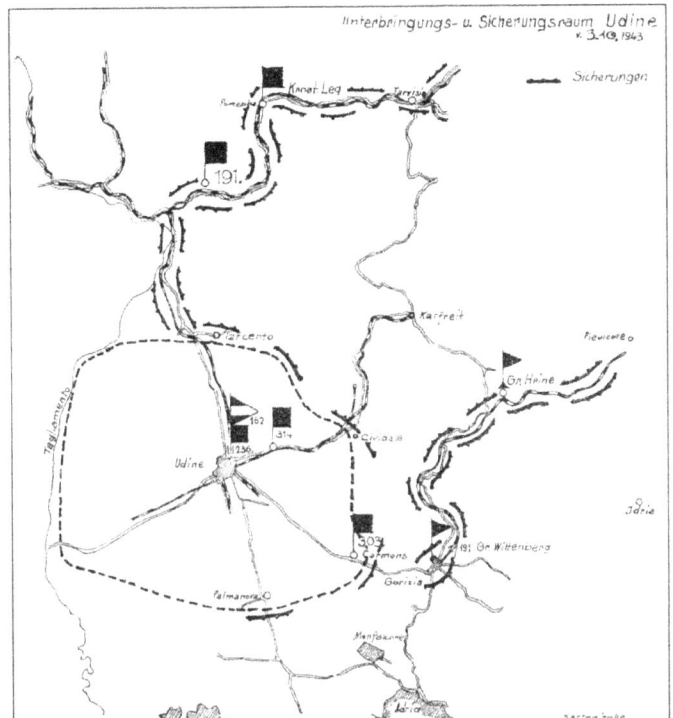

Left, the operational area of the *162.(Turk.)Inf.Div.* in the Udine area in October 1943. Right, a volunteer from Turkistan, autumn 1943.

Elements of the *162.(turk.)Inf.Div.* engaged in a round-up, autumn 1943.

The command of the *162.* was established in Monfalcone and the *Sich.Gruppe von le Fort* was again subordinated to it.

Turkestani units on the march, 1943.

Turkestan soldier of the *162.(Turk.)Inf.Div.*

Between 16 and 20 November, the division was engaged in a new series of anti-partisan operations. At the beginning of December, a large part of the units of the *162.(turk.)Inf.Div.* deployed in southern Friuli and Gorizia were transferred to the province of Ljubljana, where the activity of the partisan bands had intensified again. In particular, the units were quartered in the area between the localities of Planina (where the divisional staff was established) and Kočevje.

The battle for Kočevje

In Kočevje, south-east of Ljubljana, there was a garrison of 200-300 men, policemen of the *2.Kp./SS-Polizei-Regiment 19* and *Domobrances* of the Slovenian National Guard, under the orders of *Hauptmann der Schutzpolizei* Fridolin Guth. During the night of 9 December 1943, three Slovenian partisan brigades of the 14th Division, under the orders of Mirko Bračic, attacked the town, supported by artillery and mortar fire. The partisans managed to destroy the local mine and take most of the public buildings. However, the bulk of the garrison managed to retreat to the old Auersperg castle in the centre of the town, resisting the partisan attacks. The German command in Ljubljana was immediately alerted and organised a major force. On 10 December, *Infanterie-Regiment 314* of the *162.(turk.)Inf.Div.*, the other companies of *SS-Polizei-Regiment 19* and the *13.(verst.)Pol.Pz.Kp.*, were sent to rescue the Kočevje garrison.

General von Niedermayer, wearing coat and *Feldmütze*, with other officers and soldiers of the 162.(turk.)Inf.Div., during the march to Kočevje.

Pioneers of the 162. engaged in removing mines from the road, while marching in the direction of Kočevje, December 1943 (MNZS).

The attack was supported from above by the bombers of *Kampfgeschwader 76*. General von

Niedermayer personally led the relief column.

German tanks and soldiers penetrate into Kočevje, 12 December 1943.

Kočevje, 12 December 1943: *Hauptmann* Guth, on the left, shakes hands with General von Niedermayer, on the right, armed with a machine gun. Between the two, *SS-Obergruppenführer* Erwin Rösener, *HSSPF Alpenland*, can be glimpsed.

After passing several roadblocks during the march, prepared by other partisan forces, the column reached the town in the afternoon of 12 December, still finding the remains of the German-Slovenian garrison barricaded in the old castle. The German and, in particular, Turkestani troops, were engaged in fierce fighting in the streets of the town, forcing the partisans to retreat into the nearby forests. At the end of the fighting, at least a hundred partisans were killed and another forty were captured.

New tasks

In December 1943, the division was placed to garrison northern Italy as part of the *II. SS-Panzer-Korps*, which in turn depended on the *14. Armee* (HG C), of *Generaloberst* Eberhard von Mackensen. In January 1944, the unit was then assigned to *Oberbefehlshaber Süd* in Liguria. The division was placed in reserve, but with tasks of garrisoning and fighting partisan bands. Neiedermayer's troops actually continued their training, taking part in anti-partisan operations only rarely: at the end of 1943, the unit was judged ready for garrison duties and in March 1944, it was decided to transfer the division to Liguria as a reserve of the *Oberbefehlshaber* Süd.

Turkmen soldiers in training, 1943.

Artillerymen of the *162. (Turk.) Infanterie-Division*.

Officers of the *162.(Turk.)Inf.Div.* at a ceremony.

In Liguria, the Turkmens were employed as a coastal defence unit and anti-Partisan garrison. A few days after their arrival in Liguria, on 22 March, a US assault unit made up of Italian-Americans had landed overnight on the coast near Bonassola, with the aim of blowing up a railway tunnel to

Oskar von Niedermayer.

Generalleutnant Ralph von Heygendorff.

interrupt railway communications between Liguria and Tuscany (*mission Ginny II*); a fisherman in the area, noticing dinghies on the beach, alerted the GNR: the Axis units on the Ligurian coast went into a state of alarm, and the *162.* used as a coastal defence unit, began search operations to locate and capture the saboteurs. On 24 March, the Americans were captured by a group of G.N.R. militiamen and a German patrol; two days later, after being interrogated, the fifteen prisoners were handed over to the army, despite the fact that they were wearing their uniforms regularly; for this crime, General Anton Dostler was shot after the war.

In the meantime, due to some logistical problems, General Niedermayer's division found itself short of artillery pieces, and was therefore equipped with heavy artillery pieces of Italian origin captured from the Germans after 8 September 1943: these consisted of six 105mm batteries and two 150mm batteries, with Italian personnel, seconded from units of the Republican Army; the Italians assigned to the *162.* were incorporated into the division, wearing the German uniform with a tricolour badge on the left arm (unfortunately, there is no photographic evidence of this detail).

In May 1944, General Niedermayer was dismissed from command of the *162.(Turk.)Inf.Div.* because of opinions that conflicted with Hitler's policy: the general had declared his opposition to the brutal treatment of the populations of the occupied eastern territories and believed that the war was now compromised because of the decisions, which he considered to be insane, taken by the *Führer*·*Generalmajor* Oskar von Niedermayer was therefore replaced by *Generalleutnant* Ralph von Heygendorff, who had held the post of German military attaché in Moscow before the war.

At war with the Allies

Until May of the same year, the *162.* remained in Liguria, where it was framed in the

The Axis Forces

LXXV. *Armeekorps*. This corps had been created in Italy in March 1944, in the sector of *Heeresgruppe* C, employing *the Generalkommando des LXXXVII.Armeekorps* in *Operationszone "Alpenvorland"* (elements 278.ID). After the latter was transferred to the *Operationszone "Adriatisches Küstenland"* (*Alarm-Rgt Brandenburg*), in June, the 162nd Division, now commanded by *Generalleutnant* Ralph von Heygendorff, transferred to the *XIV.Panzerkorps* of the 14.*Armee* (*Heeresgruppe* C).

Azerbaijani volunteers framed in the *162.(Turk.)Inf.Div.*, spring 1944.

Kesserling and von Senger.

In the course of the month, the *162.* was reinforced by *Schwere Panzer-Abteilung* 504 and placed in reserve in the area of Orvieto, Umbria. For Heygendorff's unit, this was the first real baptism of fire at the front against regular Allied troops.

Due to the collapse of the Anzio and Cassino fronts. the situation in central Italy had become tremendously complicated for the German troops. Field Marshal Kesselring, in order to prevent the collapse and to coordinate the retreat towards the provisional defence lines of the Trasimeno and Arno rivers and then towards the definitive Gothic line (*Grünenline*), was forced to also employ second-line units such as the *Turkistan* that had no combat experience against regular troops.

The baptism of fire for the *162.* came on 12 June 1944, when the Turkmen units were placed at the disposal of the *14th Panzer Korps* of *General der Panzertruppe* Frido von Senger und Etterlin. On 22 June 1944, the British Eighth Army attacked the German lines on the shores of Lake Trasimeno: the Allies, after intercepting and deciphering German communications, had learned that the *162. 'Turkistan'*, considered a military unit of rather modest quality, had been deployed in that area.

Dislocation of German forces in north-central Italy on 1 July 1944. The position of the *162.* is to the right of the *19. LW-Feld-Division*.

Legionnaire of the *162.(Turk)Inf.Division*.

The British then decided to concentrate their efforts towards that very sector. The attack was fierce and on 24 June, the *162.* lost contact with the *3. Panzergrenadier-Division*, which was deployed on its right flank; the situation continued to become critical, but the Turkmen troops managed to disengage and retreat in good order to the north. On 27 June, they were able to rejoin the units of the *19th Luftwaffe-Feld-Division* and establish a line of resistance on the banks of the Cecina River, a few kilometres from Saline.

On 30 June, Field Marshal Kesselring decided to withdraw *162* from the front. Many historians believe that this was decided because of the division's poor record, although US Colonel J. H. Hougen in his '*The Story of the Famous 34th Infantry Division*', published in Arlington in 1949,

Turkestan Legionnaire. On his right arm he wears the 1st type of the Turkestan Legion's shield with the inscription 'BIZ ALLA BILEN' (With God, We Do God's Will).

General Heinrich von Vietinghoff, left in the photo, in conversation with Field Marshal Kesselring.

recalled how the Turkmen were repeatedly and violently attacked by the Allied units because they were considered the weak link in the front: but in spite of this, an actual collapse of the line held by the *162.* did not occur. Although it came close to the collapse of the line, this was finally avoided thanks to the order in which the Turkmen troops were able to withdraw.

On 25 August 1944, the Battle of Rimini began. The *162. Turkistan* had been deployed in reserve, north of Rimini; a few weeks earlier, *Oberstleutnant* Christiani, commander of *Infanterie-Regiment 303*, had proposed a plan to occupy the small, neutral state of San Marino, however, the command did not approve the operation.

On 4 September 1944, the division was deployed against the British on the Gemmano ridge and at Coriano, but this time the unit performed poorly: many Turkmen soldiers were taken prisoner by British and Canadian troops.

On 17 September, von Vietinghoff sent a secret report to Marshal Kesselring in which he reviewed the situation, writing: '*The great enemy offensive is increasingly manifesting itself as a battle of means and attrition of the first order. Our losses since 25 August are approximately 14,000*

The Axis Forces

A *PzKpfw.IV* abandoned by the Germans during the battle for Rimini, August 1944.

A German anti-tank piece engaged against Allied tanks in the Rimini sector, September 1944.

front-line fighters. The opponent has so far employed the strength of 9 divisions, including armoured divisions, and 4 armoured brigades. Since the enemy divisions are generally a third stronger than ours, they must be calculated as 12 of ours. Added to this is the complete mastery of the skies by the enemy air force (...) the carpet bombing, the grazing assaults by fighter-bombers, the constant observation from above of the fighting ground, the direction of artillery fire and tank attacks, the impossibility of any German movement during the day, the curtains of smoke and fog and, not to be overlooked the psychological impact of air warfare on ground combat, an impact that doubles the enemy's impact force so that our 8 divisions instead of facing 12 enemy divisions must in essence face 20/24 divisions and 4 armoured brigades, fed by an almost inexhaustible flow of means and men'.

Vietinghoff wrote that the battle proved to be one of the bloodiest ever fought in Italy. Both the British and the Germans had daily losses in the order of a thousand men dead, wounded and missing. On 19 September, the Allied attack was unleashed on the entire front, from Rimini to San Marino, prepared by a frightful aerial and naval land bombardment. The Chief of Staff of the LXXVI *Korps*, Runkel, said in a telephone call to Kesselring's Chief of Staff, Rottinger: "...*I saw it with my own eyes. It was like being at the Nuremberg* celebrations", referring to the nightly torchlight processions of the National Socialist Party celebrations. The focal point of the fight was the Covignano hill, attacked by two Canadian brigades and defended by the two regiments of the *29th Panzergrenadier-Division*, which acted as *whale cues* for the men of the *162. 'Turkistan'*, deployed in the centre of the *Panzergrenadier* deployment at St. Fortunato[3]. Peter Tompkins, OSS agent, pointed to the sector held by the Turkmen as the weak point of the Germanic deployment. On 14 September, the Coriano ridge was now in Allied hands, General Gerhard Muhm, then a lieutenant, stated that 162. *Turkistan* had caused the collapse of the German defences: the Turkmen, in a state of shock as a result of the violent bombardment they had suffered, largely fled or surrendered. An entire regiment, *the 314*. dissolved during the fighting at San Fortunato.

Turkmen legionaries busy preparing their ration, autumn 1944.

Legionnaire of the *162.(Turk)Inf.Div*.

During the retreat and occupation of Bellaria by the New Zealand 2nd Armoured Division, 123 more Turkmen were taken prisoner. However, along the Adriatica Romea (code name 'Black Diamond') paratroopers and Turkmen resisted hard. On the Rubicone, another 20 men of the *162* were taken prisoner. On 21 September, the Allied forces finally entered Rimini; the battle for the *Yellow Line* was over. The remains of *162.* were deployed in reconstitution in the Ravenna area.

In early October, the German Command decided to deploy the division no longer at the front, but in the rear as an anti-partisan unit. In November 1944, what remained of the *162.Turkistan-Infanterie-Division* was assigned to the Armata Liguria, under the command of Marshal Rodolfo Graziani of Italy. Deployed in the Piacenza area, the Turkmen volunteers were identified by local Italian civilians as '*Mongols*', due to their appearance. The *Turkistan* division quickly became famous in the area of Piacenza, Pavia and Parma.

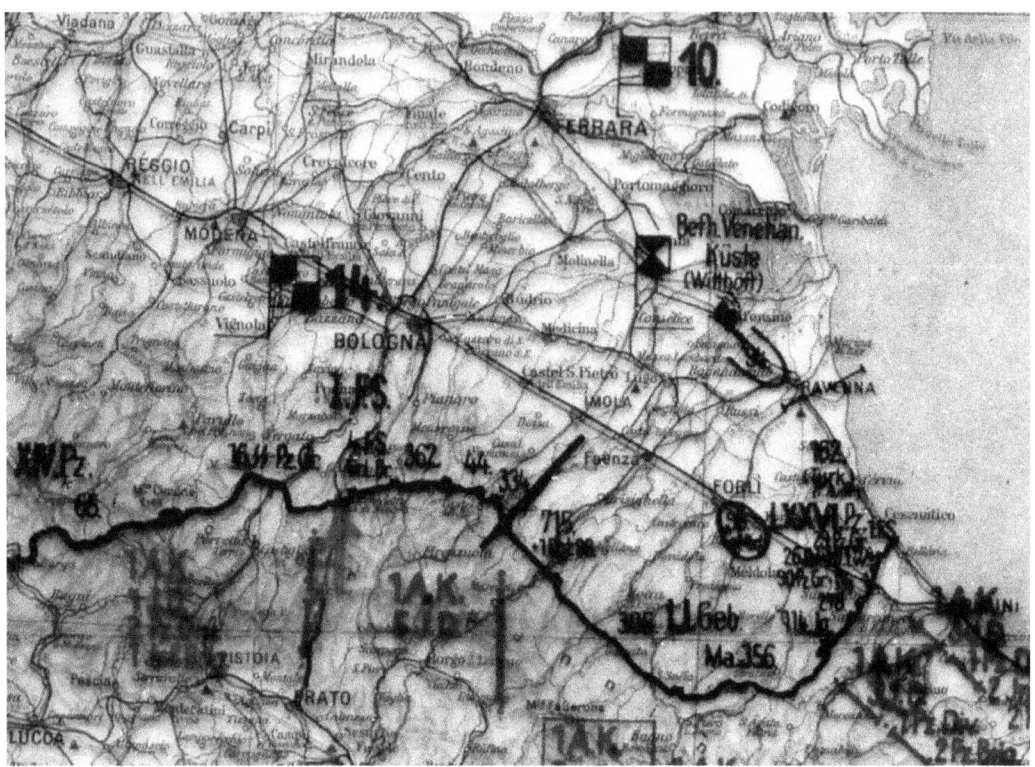

Dislocation of the German forces on the Adriatic coast at the beginning of October 1944. The *162.(Turk.)Inf.Div.* is deployed south of Ravenna.

Turkmen troops engaged in an anti-partisan operation.

Some civilians, years later, recounted how some of them were *extremely kind*, while others were exactly the opposite, unfortunately capable of committing numerous crimes against civilians.

Operations against partisan gangs

For the *Turkmen*, this was a last resort. After their poor performance at the front, the Germans would not tolerate any more missteps: if they failed even as an anti-partisan unit, the unit would be disbanded and the troops used as auxiliary units for logistical support. The units of the *162.* were then deployed in operations *Wallenstein*, *Heygerdorff*, *Regenwetter* and *Totila*. On 23 November, the *Heygendorff* operation began, in which Turkmen troops also participated: the objective was the reconquest of the mountainous areas between Piacenza and Pavia, which blocked the passage along the road connecting Piacenza and Genoa, now under partisan control. Partisan forces in that area were estimated at between 8,000 and 12,000.

The area affected by anti-partisan operations in the autumn of 1944.

Turkestan Legionnaires, 1944.

Partisan morale at that particular time was low, as General Alexander had proclaimed the suspension of all activity against the Germans and RSI soldiers for the winter. The operation began with a violent artillery barrage: the Turkmen troops attacked from Casteggio and Castel San Giovanni, advancing towards Bobbio. In the course of the action, the Turkestani troops were guilty of various crimes, including the rape of women, although the figure of 402 rapes that Resistance historiography attributes to the *Hiwis* of 162. in the Apennines of Piacenza, is only the result of post-war propaganda that took as a model the crimes of Moroccan *goumiers* in Lower Lazio. There were certainly cases of rape, but in the order of less than a dozen, immediately repressed with the execution of those responsible[4]. The operation went ahead, the Italian troops of the RSI, Italian SS, GNR and Black Brigades recaptured the castle of Zavattarello on 24 November.

The Axis Forces

A Turkmen legionnaire armed with a *PPSh 41*.

Turkestan legionnaires pose for a photo, 1944.

Between Bobbio and the Italian-German troops stood Fausto Cossu's *Justice and Freedom* Division[5]. On 27 November, the troops of the *162.(Turk.).Inf.Div.* overwhelmed the defences of the yellow partisans and managed to occupy the Penice pass, thus freeing the way to Bobbio. The parish priest of Bobbio, Francesco Bertoglio, asked the partisans not to turn the town into a Stalingrad, especially for fear of reprisals from the feared *Mongols*, so the yellow partisans decided to abandon the town and flee to the mountains. On 28 November, Bobbio fell into the hands of the Italo-Germans, thus putting an end to Operation *Heygendorff*.

Having settled the situation in the Oltrepo' Pavese, the next target of the anti-partisan operations was the town of Bettola, some thirty kilometres from Bobbio in the Arda valley. The 162. *Turkistan* started to move towards the target as early as 29 November; the days became increasingly foggy and this slowed down the operations. However, the Turkmen managed to use this factor to their advantage and on 4 December, Turkmen troops infiltrated the positions held by the partisans thanks to the weather conditions, without the latter noticing. The strongholds held by the partisans thus fell one by one into the hands of the Turkmen: the *Turkistan* troops in most cases managed to surprise the enemy, precluding any possibility of defence or reaction. On 9 December, the now defeated and decimated partisan forces retreated, forming a last small pocket of resistance between the Nure, Ceno and Aveto valleys. The report on the counter-guerrilla operations conducted by the *162. Turkistan* this time was positive, according to the German officers the troops had behaved well and had managed to influence the outcome of the operations: the idea of disbanding the unit was therefore abandoned.

German and Turkmen soldiers of the *162.(Turk.)Inf.Div.* pose for a photo in a tavern in the province of Piacenza, autumn 1944.

Von Heygendorff hands over some decorations, 1944.

In December 1944, partisan activity was extremely limited, between Alexander's proclamation, the recent defeats and the less than favourable climate, the only actions were limited to the sabotage of communication and logistical lines. On 6 January 1945, the German Command launched a new offensive against the last areas held by the partisans between the valleys in the triangle of Genoa, Piacenza and Parma. Also this time, the 162. *Turkistan* participated in the operations; its troops advanced from the Crociglia pass towards Cornolo (Parma), while the partisans preferred to retreat and offer no resistance. On 7 January, near Rocchetta di Morfasso, a Turkmen unit was ambushed by the partisans: the fighting was particularly bloody, and at the end of the day the men of the *162.* overcame the rebels thanks in part to their numerical superiority.

On 10 January 1945, the partisan forces began to disperse to avoid being annihilated and during this operation, the Turkmen forces carried out several summary executions: some of the victims were civilians mistaken for partisans or their flankers. On that same day, a squad of Turkmen crossed paths between Vianino and the valley floor with a large group of communist partisans belonging to the 31st (32nd) Garibaldi Brigade, to which some renegades from Varano de' Melegari (lower Ceno Valley, in the province of Parma) had joined. The Turkmens easily overpowered the band, then continued to rake northwards. A few days later, a vast combing took place in the Reggio area, between Scandiano and Baiso (between Sassuolo and Reggio Emilia), in which the Turkestan legionaries again operated. In his war diary, General Guido Monardi of the National Republican Army noted: '*The guerrillas pushed by the units of the* Türkestan *division withdrew precipitously, camouflaging themselves among the civilian population*'. By mid-January, the partisan forces had been defeated and dispersed, the survivors managed to find refuge in the Parma mountains, but the large partisan free zone had by then been reoccupied by Italian-German forces. In the course of these operations, three German Crosses *in Gold, Deutsches Kreuz in Gold*, were awarded to testify to the hardness of the struggle: to *Major* Konrad Bahr, *Hauptmann* Horst Külken and Heinz Dierker; another *Deutsches Kreuz* was awarded to *Generalleutnant* Ralph von Heygendorff on 30 April 1945. All this shows that the bad reputation of the *162.* was somewhat inflated after the war. In February, the *162.* performed garrison duties and defence of lines of communication but there were no major firefights and no noteworthy operations. Fate, however, was about to doom *the Turkistan* soldiers: the Allies agreed with the USSR authorities to hand over any prisoners of Soviet origin and for the Turkmen this meant immediate execution as soon as they were handed

Turkestan Legionnaire.

Legionaries from Turkestan, sharing the ration.

over to Stalin's men. Soviet law in fact provided for ten years of deportation for those who fell prisoner, and death, for those who collaborated with the *fascist enemy*, in addition to imprisonment of the entire family. As if this were not enough, on 23 February 1945, Turkey declared war on Germany, albeit only nominally. The news did not take long to reach the Turkmen, who, being Turkic in language and culture, still had a very strong cultural and above all spiritual bond (*Panturanism*, the union of all Turkic peoples from Anatolia to Central Asia) with their spiritual homeland that had declared war on the nation they were fighting for. This provoked a moral crisis in some soldiers who preferred to desert and take refuge in the mountains while waiting for the conflict to end, while others joined the partisans.

Latest tasks

On 2 March 1945, the 162. *Turkistan Infanterie-Division* was sent back to the front line. Given the now critical situation, the German troop command in Italy preferred to deploy most of the large units at the front, in anticipation of a new retreat to the Alps. In spite of the desertion of a few hundred men who had joined the partisans, the unit continued to exist and operate, albeit with a now extremely low morale. Around April, the partisans began to descend from the Parma mountains, and with them the Turkmen deserters. A few days later, they attacked Bettola, garrisoned by a detachment of Italian SS men from the *Debica* battalion. After three days of fighting, the Italian grenadiers of the 29. began to retreat, leaving Bettola in the hands of the partisans. The 162. *Turkistan*, moved to the Ferrara area to defend the eastern offshoot of the *Genghis Khan* Line, was on the line between Porto Garibaldi and Comacchio at the time of the final Allied offensive; on 3 April, the British and Italians of the *Cremona* Combat Group succeeded in taking 800 Turkmen prisoners who offered no resistance. On 21 April, after having succeeded in blocking the enemy offensive in its own sector for a few hours, the *162.* began to retreat towards Veneto, following the orders of the Germanic Command, while desertions continued: in just one day, about one hundred Azeris of *Inf.Rgt.314* deserted and surrendered to the British. Seven days later, on 28 April, after trying to cover the retreat of the German units, the division began to surrender to the Allied troops in the Padua area; a few hundred men, however, managed to avoid capture by continuing their retreat northwards. The history of the 162. *Turkistan-Infanterie-Division* officially ended on 8 May 1945, when the unit surrendered to the troops of the Eighth Army. The end of the Turkmen volunteers was sealed: they were repatriated to the USSR shortly afterwards. Ironically, the same fate befell the deserters who had joined the Italian partisans. From Taranto, a few thousand Turkmen prisoners of war were repatriated by sea to Odessa, Crimea, where Stalinist firing squads or, in luckier cases, concentration camps awaited them.

Notes

[1] The *Ostlegionen* were *Wehrmacht* units composed of Soviet prisoners or deserters; most of them served on the Western Front with tasks of coastal defence, garrison and anti-partisan operations. Some units also fought in Normandy against the Allies during Operation *Overlord*.

[2] The general ended up being court-martialled, where he avoided the death penalty thanks to the intervention of numerous officers and hierarchs, including Himmler, who testified in his favour. Nevertheless, the general was imprisoned in the Torgau fortress until the end of the conflict. A year later, when the war was over, he was arrested by the Red Army, and was taken to Moscow, where he was sentenced to 25 years of hard labour for war crimes; having fallen ill with tuberculosis, Niedermayer died in captivity on 25 September 1948.

(3) P. Romeo di Colloredo Mels, *Kesselring, a military biography, II, 1944-1960*, forthcoming.
(4) P. Romeo di Colloredo, *'Goumiers'*, Bergamo 2018, p.79 n.87.
(5) Fausto Cossu, born in Tempio Pausania in Sardinia on 25 May 1914, was an officer in the Royal Carabinieri, in 1942 he took part in war operations in Yugoslavia. Captured by the German military following the Italian armistice, he managed to escape, reached the area of Piacenza and organised a partisan formation called the *'Compagnia Carabinieri Patrioti'* (*Patriot Carabinieri Company*), quickly the formation grew in number until it became a division that took the name *'Giustizia e Libertà'* (*Justice and Freedom*). In the summer of 1944, with the help of other partisan formations, he succeeded in keeping the municipality of Bobbio and the surrounding areas under control, forcing the German command to set up a military operation to reconquer the territories that had come under partisan control. After the war, he took up the profession of lawyer and in 1999 the Municipality of Piacenza awarded him a Gold Medal of Merit. He died in Piacenza on 16 April 2005.

Bibliography

Abramian, Eduard. *Forgotten Legion: Sonderverbände Bergmann in World War II 1941-1945*. Bayside, NY:, 2007

Afiero, M. *I volontari stranieri di Hitler*, Milano, 2001

Andican, A. Ahat. *Turkestan Struggle Abroad. From Jadidism to Independence*. Haarlem, 2007

Borsarello, J. e W. Palinkx. *Wehrmacht and SS: Caucasian, Muslim, Asian Troops*. Bayeux, 2007

Caroe, Olaf. *Soviet Empire: The Turks of Central Asia and Stalinism*. London: Macmillan, 1967

De Cordier, Bruno. "*The Fedayeen of the Reich: Muslims, Islam and Collaborationism During World War II*", China and Eurasia Forum Quarterly, Vol. 8, No. 1 (2010) pp. 23-46.

Jurado, Carlos Caballero e Antony Lyles. *Foreign Volunteers of the Wehrmacht 1941-45*. Oxford, 1983

Landau, Jacob. *Pan Turkism. From Irredentism to Cooperation*. Bloomington, 1995

Littlejohn, David. *Foreign Legions of the Third Reich*. Volume 4. San Jose, 1987

Montemaggi, Amedeo. *Rimini San Marino'44. La Battaglia della Linea Gialla*. San Marino, 1983

Muñoz, Antonio J. *The East came West. Muslim, Hindu, and Buddhist Volunteers in the German Armed Forces 1941-1945*.

Muñoz, Antonio J. *Hitler's Muslims. Muslim Volunteers in Hitler's Armies, 1941-1945*. Bayside, 2007

Muñoz, Antonio J. e Oleg V. Romanko. *Hitler's White Russians. Collaboration, Extermination and Antipartisan Warfare in Byelorussia 1941-1944*. New York, 2003

Muñoz, Antonio J. *Hitler's Muslims. Muslim Volunteers in Hitler's Armies, 1941-1945*. Bayside, 2007

Ready, Lee J. *The Forgotten Axis: Germany's Partners and Foreign Volunteers in World War II*. Jefferson, 1987

Thomas, Nigel e Stephen Andrew. *The German Army 1939-45 (5): Western Front 1943-45*. Oxford, 2000

Paolo A. Dossena, "*Hitlers Turkestani Soldiers: A History of the 162nd Turkistan Infantry Division*" Helion & Co Ltd

Raffaele Moncada, "*Ordine di Kesselring: «Arretrare combattendo»: La battaglia d'inseguimento a nord di Roma. Giugno 1944*" Ugo Mursia Editore

Nigel Thomas, "*The German Army 1939–45 (5): Western Front 1943–45*" Osprey Publishing

DEUTSCHE TRUPPEN IN ITALIEN, la Repubblica Sociale Italiana e la 'Turkistan Division' 1943-1945, volume II, Museo per la Fotografia e la Comunicazione Visiva di Piacenza.

The SS 'Debica' Battalion
SS-Freiwilligen Bataillon 'Debica'
by Leonardo Sandri

Major Guido Fortunato in Münsingen in November 1943.

The *Debica* Battalion constituted the elite unit of the Italian Armed SS Units, better known as the Italian SS Legion. Formed in November 1943 with volunteers who had agreed to be recruited into the *Waffen SS* to fight on all fronts except Italy, it was then transferred to Italy where, apart from a brief interlude in June 1944 when it fought north of Rome against the Anglo-Americans, it took part as a leading unit in some of the major anti-guerrilla operations that affected Piedmont and the Piacenza area, inflicting heavy losses on the gangs, particularly in the Lanzo Valleys and Valdossola, at the cost of negligible casualties, some twenty casualties in all.

Constitution and Training in Poland

The SS *Debica* (read Debiza) Battalion, the unofficial name of what was to become the elite unit of the Italian SS Legion, was born on 11 November 1943 at the Münsingen training camp, where about 10,000 Italian soldiers of all specialities had been gathered, who had expressed their willingness to continue fighting alongside the Third Reich in the *Waffen SS* since the first days after 8 September. On 10 November, all the Italian volunteers, in view of their departure for Italy, were gathered on the square of the training camp where it was announced to them that a special battalion of volunteers was being formed that would fight on all fronts, except the Italian one, framed in German units of the *Waffen SS*[1]. The creator of the formation of this special battalion, which took on the initial name of *Italienisches* SS *Freiwilligen Bataillon* (Italian SS Volunteer Battalion), was Bersaglieri Major Guido Fortunato, who had commanded the 19th Battalion of the 6th Bersaglieri Regiment on the Russian front where he had been decorated by the Germans with the Iron Cross of 1st and 2nd Class. Major Fortunato, seeing the negative atmosphere prevailing at the Münsingen training camp where alongside volunteers motivated and

Volunteers of the Armed Militia lined up in front of the barracks of the Münsingen (BA) polygon.

determined to continue fighting against the Anglo-Americans, in addition to false volunteers, many former inmates of the military prisons who had escaped after 8 September, agreed with the small *Waffen SS* command, which supervised the formation of what was initially called Milizia Armata and would later become the Italian SS Legion, to personally select the most motivated, preferably decorated, Italian soldiers from the mass of soldiers, who would form a special battalion through a strict selection process. Eventually, 20 officers and 570 non-commissioned officers and troopers were selected and transferred to the nearby training camp in Feldstetten, located some ten kilometres east of Münsingen.

Münsingen October 1943. From the right, Major Guido Fortunato, *SS-Hstuf.* Thaler (centre) and an officer of the Armed Militia.

Those who did not pass the selection formed a marching battalion, placed under the orders of Major Nicasio Cordoni, which returned to Italy at the beginning of December, where the other battalions of the Armed Militia were already located. On 5 December 1943, the battalion left Feldstetten by train for Poland, via Vienna - Prague; after a few days' journey it reached the village of Kockanowka and then continued on minor lines to Debica in south-eastern Poland, where it arrived on the 14th of the same month to carry out a training period of a couple of months at the *Waffen SS* Training Camp Heidelager, located near the village of P'skow, about 12 km north-east of Debica, from which the battalion took its name.

Heidelager (Poland), December 1943. The twenty officers of the SS *Debica* Battalion with two German instructors. The coats are those of the *Waffen SS* while the berets are still those of the original units.

From left, Corporal Antonio Stormi, Sergeant Mario Mullon and Corporal Mark.

In addition to the Italian volunteers who were housed in Sector III (Ring III), the 20th *Waffen SS* Division, composed of Estonians, was also at the training camp at that time. During their three months in Poland, the Italian volunteers did not undergo any special training nor were they provided with new German uniforms, so much so that they had to make do as best they could to withstand the harsh Polish winter climate. This is what is written in Corporal Antonio Stormi's diary about the establishment of the battalion and the training period in Poland: '*19 September 1943: A ray of sunshine shines on our path again. Today the German comrades have offered us the chance to take up arms again, to continue the war with honour. Italy rises again!*

The Axis Forces

Two senior officers of the Armed Militia in a photo taken in Münsingen.

Mussolini freed from his captivity by German paratroopers, regained power. The new state, the Italian Social Republic, came back to life. Unfortunately, in the days immediately following the armistice, every thing, body, state and military office that had been, was destroyed, erased from national life. We must start again from scratch. It will be difficult and hard, but we will succeed. 2 November 1943: We are in Munsingen (Ulm). Here, the German Command has gathered most of the Italians who are returning to wear a uniform and to fight. There will be about 10,000 of us. We await our fate with confidence. We do not want anything. We only wish to continue our war alongside the Germans. We want to fight. To fight and die for our Italy. 10 November 1943: At the last moment, while the units are already preparing to leave for Italy, the last assembly takes place. Those who want to join a special battalion are asked. Purpose of the battalion: to go on all fronts, minus the Italian one. Prize: death in combat. I feel an invisible hand pushing me. I accept without hesitation. Major Fortunato, who chooses the elements, gives me a stern look. I fear for a moment that I will not be chosen. But I see with joy that the major points me to the side where the enlisted men are standing.15 November 1943: First days in the battalion. Life is going well. Great enthusiasm among the battalion members.

Estonian *Waffen-SS* volunteers in training at the Heidelager camp with mortar and *MG-34* (*Reimo Leol Collection*).

We await our fate with understandable anxiety. Where shall we go? When? 2 December 1943: The days pass and we are still here: The other departments have long since left for their destinations. Some will already be at the front or being rounded up. We, on the other hand, are always here, doing nothing, inactive. 5 December 1943: It seems that our fate has finally been decided. We leave today for Poland where we will do our education in an SS camp.10 December 1943: On our way to Poland. The days pass slowly. But why do we go so slowly? After two months of waiting we long to start our education soon so that we will soon be ready.

The entrance to the Heidelager camp, 1944.

SS units in training at the Heidelager camp.

An Italian soldier surrenders himself to a German unit on the Balkan front after 8 September 1943 (BA).

14 December 1943: We arrived in Heidelager the day before yesterday. Having bathed, we were housed in nice little barracks at the III Ring. We were told that today or tomorrow we should have our new uniforms with weapons so that we could start our training immediately. 20 December 1943: We are still at the same point. Words, words, words. We have had neither weapons nor clothes and we are always inactive. But have they forgotten that this battalion exists? 25 December 1943: Fourth Christmas of the war. In my dormitory we made a beautiful tree. Adorned with makeshift means, bits of paper, a few candles stolen who knows where, it looks beautiful. Perhaps because we have all done our utmost to make it shiny and rich; and perhaps because it reminds us of other trees, made in other times, in the intimacy of family. In the evening, we all gather together around the tree. We watch mute as the candles burn, almost shy. Then a slow song quietly rises in the room. It is a sweet, melodious, peaceful song. Almost a mystical atmosphere reigns in the room. We sing softly, softly and look into each other's eyes. We are men and soldiers. But the tears fall, also slowly, slowly on our pensive faces. 2 January 1944: Life goes on; life in the new year. What will fate have in store for us? Will we see the end of the war? Will we see our Victory ? Mute questions to which the heart replies mute and foreboding. Victory, Victory, Italy. The name of the Fatherland rings in our ears, punctuated by heartbeats. We are even obsessed by these hopes. For now we, unfortunately, are always here inoperative. Others are already doing their duty and have begun the reconstruction of the new state. When will we also do something?".

This is the testimony of Sergeant Angelo Camisa: *'Before 8 September 1943, I was in Greece and was a member of the 18th Artillery Regiment. At the time of the armistice I was taken* prisoner by the Germans and taken by them to Holland to the 9th Stammlager where there were also Russian prisoners. After a few days a German officer came and harangued the Italian soldiers, all lined up in a large shed, to urge them to enlist in the German army but without much success. After a few days he renewed the exhortation, then an Italian non-commissioned officer came out of the ranks expressing his desire to fight the Anglo-Americans but in an Italian uniform. There were several volunteers including myself who were isolated from the others and were sent to Munsingen to a training camp. Here Major Fortunato came after a few days, dressed as an SS major, to enlist volunteers for the Russian front. He wanted a select unit with people over 5'7" tall and with high physical requirements, so there were only a few selected. I accepted the invitation and with the other selected I was sent to the Debica camp in Poland where we were given a lot of food and liquor compared to Münsingen, on liberty we behaved a bit lively thanks to the fact that we wore the Italian uniform. In February 1944, we returned to Italy without any training'.

Italian volunteers sent to a recruitment centre by a German soldier (*Signal* magazine).

SS and Police Captain Friedrich Noweck.

The return to Italy and the first anti-guerrilla operations

On 12 February 1944, the battalion was loaded onto a train convoy to return to Italy, reaching the Brenner Pass on the 20th and Milan on the 21st. After a brief stop at the Adriatica barracks in Bicocca, where the battalion was structured into four rifle companies[2], each with four platoons, and distributed weapons including some

Another photo of Captain Friedrich Noweck.

Captain Arturo Dal Dosso.

heavy machine guns, two squads with four weapons per company but no mortars, the *Debica* then reached Pinerolo on 23 February where, with the various battalions of the Milizia Armata, the 1st Assault Brigade of the Italian Volunteer Legions[3] was being set up In Pinerolo, *the Debica* was stationed at the *Principe Amedeo* barracks, former headquarters of the Royal Army Cavalry School[4]. The 1st Assault Brigade was not yet a unit within the *Waffen SS,* of which it bore no designation, only the battalion that arrived from Poland was from the beginning considered to all intents and purposes part of the *Waffen SS*, both as a designation, *SS-Freiwilligen Bataillon*, as well as wearing the black insignia without the rune[5], although many bore the SS runes with the complacency of the German education and liaison officer at the battalion, SS Captain and Police Captain Friedrich Noweck. Noweck proved to be an officer who was very close to the Italian volunteers of the *Debica*, so much so that the battalion often operated as an autonomous unit detached from the brigade hierarchy. Noweck, who was born in Danzig in 1914, had taken part in the Polish company in the 1st Danzig Infantry Regiment. On 15 October 1939, he had transferred to the *Polizei* Division of the *Waffen SS* as a non-commissioned officer platoon commander. From 1 January to 13 July 1940, he had attended the officer's cadet course at the Berlin-Kopenick police academy and was promoted to the rank of second lieutenant. He then held the post of company commander in the Pelplin police battalion until 15 September 1940 and thereafter, until 30 June 1942, he held the post of instructor officer at the Pelplin police academy. From 1 July to 4 December 1942, he had served as an anti-tank warfare instructor officer at the police school in Den Hag. From 5 December 1942 to 5 January 1944, he had fought on the Eastern Front as commander of the anti-tank company of the 13th SS Police Regiment. On 20 January 1944, he had been transferred to Italy, to Mestre, initially as an instructor officer at the I Battalion Volontari di Polizia Italia (*I.Polizei*

SS-Brigdf. **Peter Hansen.**

Val Pellice, March 1944: an AB 41 armoured car of *Pz.Abt.208* **during the** *'Spärber'* **operation .**

Freiwilligen Bataillon Italien) and later assigned to *Debica*. In the course of the conflict, the officer had been decorated with the Iron Cross 2nd Class on 5.9.39, the Danzig Cross in November 1939, the Cross of War Merit 2nd Class in February 1943, the Iron Cross 1st Class on 21.5.43, the Infantry Assault Badge on 12.12.43 and the Wounded in Black Badge in December 1943. In addition to Noweck, SS Police Captain Kohlstedt, later replaced by Second Lieutenant von Kőbl, was assigned to the battalion as an officer in the administration, and a couple of non-commissioned officers per company completed the German staff assigned to the battalion. When the battalion returned to Italy, its founder, Major Guido Fortunato, whose fate and the reasons for his dismissal from the *Waffen SS* are unknown, was no longer part of the battalion's staff; in his place, Major Emilio Sassi was appointed; the commanders of the three rifle companies were respectively Captain Roberto Cantarella[6], Captain Arturo Dal Dosso (2nd) and Captain Silvio Premuda (3rd). The Ordnance Officer was Lieutenant Tosatti, the Administration Officer was Captain Eliseo Signorini and the Medical Officer was the peer Emilio Rimini.

According to a document, known as 'Arbeitsplan Hansen' (Hansen Work Plan), named after the commander of the 1st Assault Brigade, dated 29 February 1944, the *Debica* went to form the 1st Battalion of the 1st Regiment. On 13 March, the SS volunteers were issued with new uniforms, the collarless paratrooper uniforms[7], to replace the old uniforms they had worn since 8 September. The following day, the battalion was transferred to Val Pellice, with the command and the 3rd Company in Torre Pellice, the 1st Company in Luserna San Giovanni, at the *Pettinati* barracks, and the 2nd Company and Bricherasio. Among the duties assigned to the SS volunteers, besides setting up roadblocks, was escorting trains on the Torre Pellice - Pinerolo line. According to Hansen's work plan, the *Debica* Battalion was to be deployed as follows: command and one company in Bobbio Pellice, one company in Torre Pellice and one company in Villar Pellice. However, due to the presence of numerous bands in the middle and upper Val Pellice, the battalion was dislocated at the mouth of the valley. On 21 March 1944, the *Debica* Battalion took part in Operation "Spärber" (Sparrowhawk), which mainly affected Val Luserna, Val Pellice and Val Germanasca and secondarily Val Chisone. From Torre Pellice, the *Debica* passed the Santa Margherita checkpoint and went up the valley divided into three columns: one along the road at the bottom of the valley, one halfway up the orographic left and the third along the Pellice stream.

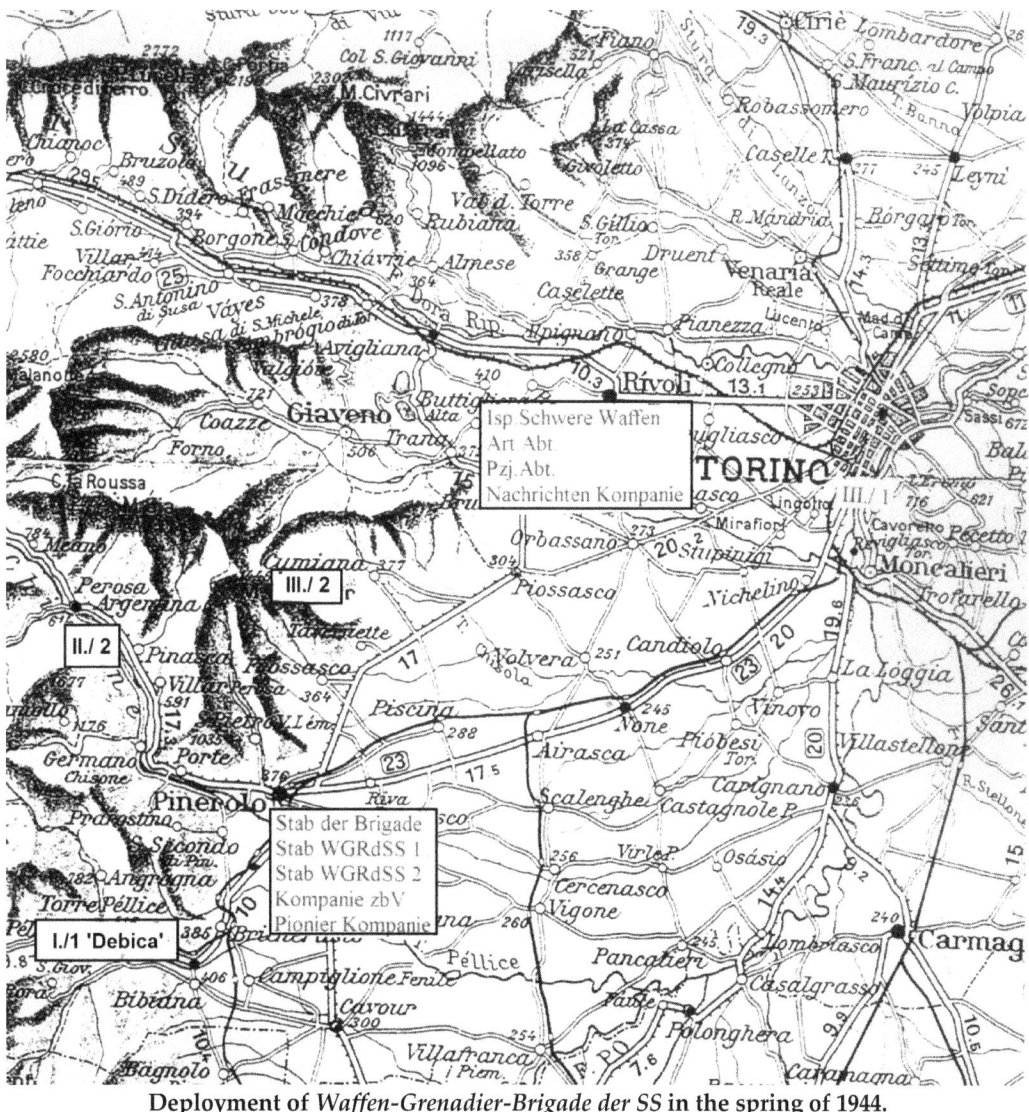

Deployment of *Waffen-Grenadier-Brigade der SS* in the spring of 1944.

During the advance on Villar Pellice the 2nd Company under the orders of Captain Arturo Dal Dosso, was attacked in the Bordella area and encircled by a group of partisans from Commander Ulisse's detachment, who were stationed on the heights on either side of the road, firing some heavy machine guns and a mortar. A mortar shell, which fell near the position from which Captain Dal Dosso was directing the attack, wounded the officer, who was hit by shrapnel in the head and chest. Wounded by machine-gun fire while crossing a stretch in the open to bring the battalion command the news that the 2nd Company was in trouble was also Lance Corporal Giovanni Fois. In the course of this fighting, *Debica* had its first two casualties, Sergeant Loris Ragoni, later decorated posthumously with the Iron Cross of the 2nd Class[8] and Lance Corporal Roberto Pizzi, also decorated with the Iron Cross of the 2nd Class in his memory[9]. In addition to Captain Arturo Dal Dosso and Lance Corporal Fois, Corporal Antonio Raggi and SS Grenadier Angelo Fusco were wounded. The wounded were all taken to the '*Maria Immacolata*' hospital in Pinerolo, Dal Dosso was awarded the Silver Wounded Badge while Lance Corporal Giovanni Fois, promoted to the rank of sergeant, was decorated with the Iron Cross of the 2nd Class[10].

San Germano Val Chisone (TO). An SS unit of the *II./2* assembled in the centre of the village after carrying out a round-up, spring 1944.

To the rescue of the 2nd Company, the 1st Company intervened, which was in turn forced to defend itself due to the violent enemy machine-gun fire. A squad of four Italian volunteers led by SS Police Sergeant Reinhard Schroders leapt to attack the position from which the partisans were firing a heavy machine gun, destroying it by throwing hand grenades. The rest of the 1st Company led by SS Police Sergeant Ludwig Schubert then managed to break through the enemy line of resistance and drive the partisans away. Three of them were killed in combat while four others, including commander Ulysses, were captured and then handed over to the army. The commander of the detachment, Ulysses, who was firing from a rock overlooking the road was overpowered by an SS man who came up behind him and fired a shot at him, killing him. Villar Pellice was then occupied in the course of the day.

This is what Corporal Antonio Stormi wrote in his diary about the day's events: '*21 March*

1944. 3.15 a.m. Sudden awakening. At last! We set off for the first raking action. Today is spring and the game begins as our song says. Strange coincidence of happy omen. At 6 o'clock we start firing. We leave the western checkpoint of Torre Pellice and advance towards Villar Pellice (8 km). The 2nd Company meets the first resistance. A partisan heavy machine gun in a bunker beats our line of march with its fire. A platoon leaves to destroy the bunker and put the partisans to flight. The first prisoner is taken to the Command Post. Upon interrogation, he denies any participation in the sabotage actions. At 10 o'clock, the 1st Company also leaves with another leader. From Luserna, through Lusernetta it heads towards Val Chisone. The boys are enthusiastic, they set off with carefree glee. Good luck!".

The *Debica*, reinforced by an 88-piece from a *Flak* unit and some armoured vehicles from the Gruppo Corazzato '*Leonessa*' (Armoured Group '*Leonessa*'), continued the combing of the Pellice Valley in the following days, occupying, without encountering organised resistance, Bobbio Pellice on 22 March and Villanova, the last village in the valley, on the 23rd. On the day of 23 March, a *Debica* column, leaving from Bobbio Pellice, descended into Val Germanasca through Colle Giuliano, putting a group of partisans stationed in Rodoretto to flight. On 24 March, a column of the battalion headed towards Prà del Torno, above Villanova, where the presence of a base of a partisan formation had been reported.

In Val Germanasca, near the Raut bridge, an armoured car of the GNR's Gruppo Corazzato '*Leonessa*' (Armoured Group '*Leonessa*') fires on the positions occupied by the partisans and advances towards Perrero.

While on the march, the SS unit came under machine-gun fire placed on a rise. Second Lieutenant Aldo Volpato with SS Police Sergeant Herbert Turner and a handful of men, and without mountain equipment, climbed a rise to a privileged position from where they set up a machine gun and attacked the enemy camp from behind, causing the death of 14 partisans and capturing eleven others, as well as a heavy machine gun, a light machine gun, eight rifles, ammunition and a large quantity of supplies. For the valour shown in this action, Sgt. of the SS Police Herbert Tuner was decorated with the Iron Cross 2nd Class.

SS-Oberführer Otto Jungkunz interrogates prisoners during an anti-partisan operation, 1944.

On 25 March 1944, operations were suspended following contacts between the Val Pellice partisan leaders and the Chief of Staff of the 1st Assault Brigade, *SS-Oberführer* Otto Jungkunz, which led to a truce in the fighting that continued until 29 March. Most of the members of the Val Pellice '*Justice and Freedom*' formations accepted the conditions set by the officer and many partisans and stragglers were thus able to return to their homes undisturbed, while others were enrolled in the Todt Organisation and some agreed to enrol in the *Debica* Battalion.

Spring 1944, Turin province: an Italian SS unit being transferred during an anti-partisan operation.

This is the testimony of one of these new 'volunteers': '*Before 8 September 1943, I was in the 'Monte Cervino' Ski Battalion. At the armistice I returned to my home in Val Chisone where I was forced to hide as a renegade. In March 1944 with others I was captured during a round-up by*

An Italian SS mountain piece in action, 1944.

soldiers belonging to the 'Debica' Battalion, whose existence I was completely unaware of. Taken to the command post with the other prisoners, I was interrogated by some officers who proposed that we enlist in the battalion or be sent to Germany. It was a German SS unit that operated quite independently of the other Italian SS units that were in the area, and we wore black insignia while the other units wore red insignia for a while. I was assigned to 1st Company.

On 29 March, the Battalion Command moved to Bobbio Pellice where the three companies were concentrated. On the same day, military operations resumed in Val Germanasca, which led to the annihilation of the "*Giustizia e Libertà*" formations still active in the area. In Perrero, the SS volunteers recovered a cache of artillery ammunition that was later transferred to the Fenestrelle fort. This is what is written in Corporal Antonio Stormi's diary on the last stages of the operation: "*29 March 1944. The actions continued day by day. Val Pellice is liberated. The Battalion Command has settled in Bobbio Pellice, the last village before the French border. Captain Prearo, leader of the bandits, accepted a meeting with Captain Noweck. He will be offered a surrender at his discretion. His men will be allowed to go down into the valley, abandoning that bandit life and return to their homes. Prearo does not yield. He demands a lot. The actions will continue. I have questioned the prisoners. And how many! To the questions put to them they answer either evasively or inaccurately. In fact, they don't even know what they were fighting for. Now they are almost glad it ended like this. Interestingly enough, a small, sordid Jew[11] tried to hide his condition. He denied being a Jew. Finally after a little boxing match he admitted it. Perhaps his face, broken in collaboration with Captain Noweck, made him think a little and remember that he was also the communist leader of a gang. Another good prey is an old and ugly Florentine professor, a subversive propagandist*'.

On 5 April, at the end of the operations, the Battalion Command returned to Torre Pellice, together with the three companies still stationed at Luserna, Bricherasio and Torre Pellice. At this date the battalion had a strength of 21 officers, 33 non-commissioned officers and 295 soldiers for a total of 349 men. This was about 200 men less than two months earlier, as many had taken advantage of their return to Italy to desert or switch to other units of the Italian Social Republic. Some passed into the ranks of the resistance, one of whom, Gian Paolo Meneghetti, preferred to shoot himself in the head at Rognosa, in the Angrogna Valley, rather than surrender when he found himself surrounded by his former comrades who recognised him and invited him to surrender, calling him by name.

The Axis Forces

Officer of the SS *Debica* Battalion, the only unit that was allowed to wear black insignia, in many cases with SS runes, from its inception (SIMONI).

Two young SS volunteers in the Debica battalion. The soldier on the right improperly wears *a Waffen SS* NCO cap.

This is the situation of the battalion in the first months after returning to Italy in the memoirs of an NCO: '*At the end of February 1944 I arrived in Pinerolo where I finally received a new uniform, a paratrooper's model without a collar, in place of mine which was still the one I wore in Greece on 8 September, completed with an overcoat that the Germans had given me. In Pinerolo I was graded into the 'Debica' Battalion, which had just arrived in Italy after a period of training in a Waffen SS camp in Poland. My placement in the battalion was completely accidental and due to the fact that I became friends with one of them, nicknamed '100 pistols', because he used to carry two or three pistols, who proposed me to a battalion officer. He proposed me to an officer of the battalion who, given my well-known characteristics, arranged for my transfer to the 'Debica'. The 'Debica' was a sui generis unit within the brigade, we wore the black SS insignia, unlike the other units, which for many months wore red insignia, so much so that we called them 'tomatoes', and it was also made up of a very small nucleus of officers and non-commissioned officers around whom the unit revolved. The German liaison officer, Captain Noweck, had great faith in the spirit of 'Debica' and ensured that the unit was not polluted by the introduction of new officers who had not trained in Poland. In the 'Debica' there was a special spirit that made it the elite department of the entire Italian SS Legion, only in the last months of the war were new officers and non-commissioned officers attached. A second lieutenant attached to my company, who immediately understood the trend that was circulating among us, told me clearly that he was the one who had to learn from us. At Pinerolo we were housed in the former cavalry barracks, the initial strength was about 500 men in four companies;*

The Axis Forces

Italian SS soldiers with a mortar, 1944.

SS-Oberfürer Karl-Heinz Burger.

I was assigned to Captain Dal Dosso's 2nd Company. Of the more than 500 who returned from Poland, a certain number deserted on their return to Italy, others went on to join units of the RSI or the brigade itself. In mid-March, the battalion moved to Val Pellice where we were employed in an operation against partisans. The companies had no mortars but only a few Breda 37 machine guns as heavy weapons. On 21 March, I was at the side of the company commander, Captain Dal Dosso, when a mortar shell hit our position, the officer and our order bearer were wounded, I escaped without injury. After this episode, Dal Dosso was always particularly nervous when we came under partisan mortar fire. In the meantime, I had been promoted to sergeant and was in charge of setting up a first squad with two 81 mortars captured from the partisans. When Dal Dosso, who had recovered from his wound, returned to the company, a friendly, defiant relationship was established between him and me about my ability to hit the enemy positions on the third shot at best. Later, when the mortar platoon was formed, I was given command of it. I preferred to move with only two pieces and load as many men as possible with ammunition because the mortar has a solitary worm and consumes a considerable amount of rounds. During this first operation in Piedmont, that particular spirit that later characterised the history of the unit had not yet formed, there were still many who had enlisted only to return to Italy, some deserted and went with the partisans. During the battalion's stay in Val Pellice, I sometimes served as a train escort along the line to Pinerolo.

Transfer to Central Italy and deployment to the Front

On 12 April 1944, the battalion was concentrated in Pinerolo where the first mortars.

On the 14th, 32 new Fiat 626 trucks and 12 motorbikes of the III Transport Column supplied by the German Gendarmerie Command in Italy arrived, with which the battalion was transferred to central Italy with a view to deployment to the southern front. The battalion left on 15 April and followed the following route: Turin - Alessandria - Bologna - Florence - Arezzo - Perugia - Spoleto, which it reached on 18 April. On the Spoleto - Assisi road, the previous day, Lance Corporal Antonino Leonardi, who was part of the group of riflemen who had left a few days earlier, was seriously wounded in an ambush with an eye. This is what is written in Corporal Antonio Stormi's diary about the battalion's transfer to central Italy: '*We leave suddenly. First destination Bologna. A crazy hope shakes my heart. Maybe we are going to the front. Of course we are not too well armed but our enthusiasm will make up for the lack of weapons. From one stage to the next without incident we arrived in Spoleto where we make a final stop. During the journey, I observed the behaviour of the population, expressionless or even hostile faces. But why, I ask myself, are they not glad, the bourgeois, that we are going to the front, that there are still Italians defending our Italy, their homes and families, their big bellies? Spoleto: dead and empty. The shops are closed, few people in the streets. The 'Jabos' (Anglo-American planes) are constantly over the city. They swoop down suddenly, unload their bombs, a machine gunshot and then off again. And so every day*'.

A *Debica* SS legionnaire armed with a *Beretta* MAB submachine gun in a village in central Italy during an anti-band operation in the spring of 1944.

It is not clear whether the battalion was destined for the front and was deployed at the last moment as an anti-bandit or whether it had already been planned to initially take part in some anti-guerrilla operations between Umbria and Marche, it is a fact that for the entire month of April, the *Debica* operated in Umbria based in Spoleto, in particular along the Via Flaminia between Spoleto and Assisi. On 26 April, the battalion took part in a vast anti-guerrilla operation under the SS and Police Commander for Central Italy, *SS-Oberfürer* Burger. The operation involved a vast area between Marche and Umbria in the area between Monte Pennino, Sorifa, Colle Croce and Passo Scheggia.

During this operation, a section of the Debica captured along the Scheggia - Gubbio road the well-known gang leader, former captain of the Royal Army, Raniero. These are the meagre notes on the operation in Corporal Antonio Stormi's diary: "*The companies leave tonight for the round-up. They go towards San Severino, Tolentino, Scheggia. The actions bore little fruit. The rebel bands have disbanded*".

The only significant action saw the 1st Company, under the orders of Captain Roberto Cantarella, which in the Scheggia area was engaged in the capture of a partisan base. Due to the intense fire, two platoons of the company sent on the attack were forced to retreat. Captain Cantarella rounded up about twenty volunteers, who led the attack and soon managed to rout the enemy. SS casualties were insignificant, only a few lightly wounded, while the partisans, in addition to suffering casualties in dead

Young SS volunteer from *Debica* during the retreat towards Florence in June 1944.

and wounded, abandoned two mortars and numerous weapons. During the operation, three men from the battalion, while combing the slopes of Monte San Vicino, lost contact with the rest of the unit due to the thick fog and took refuge in a hut where they were surprised by the partisans. Two of them, Lance Corporal Narciso Maddalena[12] and SS Grenadier Ennio Di Giulio[13] were shot, while the third, although seriously wounded and believed dead, managed to save himself. During the operational cycle in Umbria, SS Grenadier Pietro Tabarrini was reported missing in the Foligno area.

In early May, at the end of the operations, the battalion was transferred to Tolentino minus the 3rd Company, which was detached to San Severino Marche. The battalion conducted numerous patrols in the area between San Severino - Tolentino and Metelica, in particular hunting prisoners of war who had escaped from the Sforzacosta camp following an Anglo-American air raid. On 6 May, a team under the orders of Lieutenant Malanga, travelling on a truck to Cessapalombo in search of a radio transmitter in contact with the Anglo-Americans, came across a young boy who, upon escaping, was killed by a machine-gun fire fired by the officer. On 17 May, during one of these patrols, two Croatian prisoners of war and a former Italian officer were stopped near Cantiano and found armed and shot on the spot. On 31 May, the battalion left Tollentino to be

The *Oscha*. Walter Morini, platoon commander of the *Debica* 1.Kompanie in a photo of May 1944 in which he still holds the rank of *Scharführer* (MORINI).

transferred to the Latium coast north of Rome in an anti-landing role. During the night, the Debica arrived in Orvieto where it stopped. On the morning of 1 June, while the Battalion Headquarters and 2nd Company moved to Spoleto, 1st Company and 3rd Company reached the Latium coast near Palo, in the commune of Ladispoli, with 3rd Company defending Palo and a detachment at Orsini Castle and 1st Company stationed further south, both tactically attached to the *Wehrmacht* 92 Infantry Division. Here, the SS volunteers were divided into small groups of three or four men to guard the defensive preparations built in the previous months in anticipation of a possible Anglo-American landing. On 2 June, SS and Police Captain Friedrich Noweck assumed operational command of the battalion.

On 4 June, following the advance along the Lazio coast of American armoured vanguards, against which the SS volunteers could do nothing as they were completely lacking in anti-tank weapons, the order was given to retreat to Grosseto. On the same day, all positions along the coast suffered intense aerial machine-gun fire that caused the destruction of many vehicles. The order to fall back, due to the continuous aerial machine-gun fire and the total lack of transport was carried out in complete disorder and without any organisation. Each small group tried to head north on its own, only a few of the better organised nuclei made the retreat with a certain routine, often having to fight their way through as they were overtaken by American scouting units such as Marshal Walter Morini's platoon, which found itself cut off on the 5th and only thanks to the skill and cold-bloodedness of the non-commissioned officer, a veteran of many campaigns, was able to escape capture. Morini was later decorated with the Iron Cross 2nd Class[15]. In the same situation was Sergeant Major Enrico Vicentini's platoon, which eventually managed to reach the German lines unscathed. For this he was later decorated with the Cross of Merit in War with Swords of the 2nd Class[16]. Also decorated with the Cross of War Merit with Swords of 2nd Class for episodes of valour during the retreat from the Lazio coast were Marshal Fernando Vasquez[17] and Corporal Umberto Lucarelli[18]. On 5 June, the Battalion Command and the 2nd Company from Spoleto also fell back to Perugia. On 7 June, the 2nd Company was sent to the Grosseto area where the gathering point for the various battalion units in retreat was planned. Here the *Debica* was supposed to pass to the tactical dependencies of the 162nd *Turkestan* Infantry Division which, together with other German units, had the task of slowing down the Anglo-American advance between Lake Bolsena and the coast, but in fact, since it was no longer an organic unit, it was disengaged from any dependency on higher commands. The main directions of the retreat were one along the coast as far as Orbetello and the second further inland towards Monte Romano and then converging on Grosseto. During the retreat, in addition to clashes with the American armoured vanguards, the SS volunteers had to endure the constant threat of aerial machine gunfire and attacks by partisan bands. In one of the countless aerial machine-gun attacks, Captain Noweck was wounded on 10 June near Orbetello, and Lieutenant Dante Ferrarese was captured near Grosseto. After two days in captivity, he managed to free himself and rejoin the rest of the battalion.

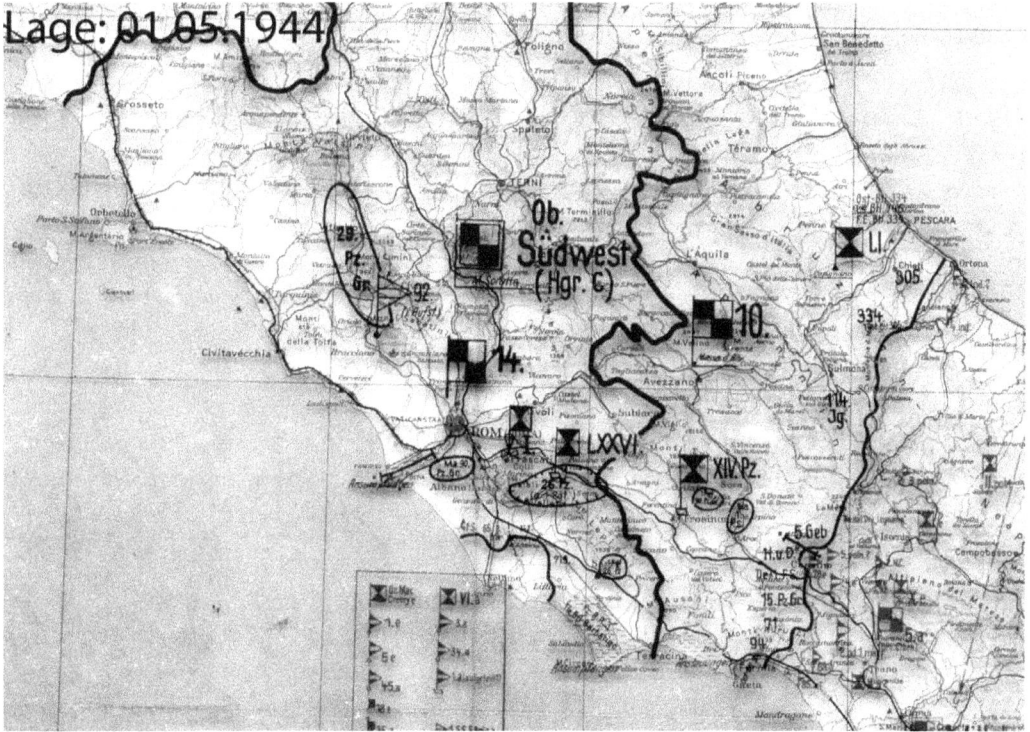

Dislocation of German forces in central Italy on 1 May 1944, the sector where the *Debica* battalion operated.

On 13 June, the Battalion Command from Perugia received the order to move to Florence where a collection point for the retreating units was set up at the Cascine Nuove. On 23 June, all those who had reached Florence were reorganised into organic divisions and transferred by rail to Emilia Romagna. On 23rd June, while the railway convoy was at a halt at the San Felice Panaro station in the Modena area, Second Lieutenant Apollinare Sassi[19], son of the battalion commander, while with other comrades was inspecting a nearby goods train loaded with damaged armoured vehicles from the front, inadvertently touched the high voltage cables, being electrocuted instantly. Because of this tragic episode, Major Sassi asked to be put on leave, which was granted, and in his place was Captain Noweck, who had remained with his unit despite his injury in Orbetello. After a brief stop in Imola, the remains of the battalion continued on to Forlinpopoli where they were housed in a former cavalry barracks, awaiting the arrival of other stragglers. This is the testimony of a NCO from *Debica* about the battalion's deployment to the front: '*On 31 May, we left for the front, reaching Spoleto again. Here the battalion was split into two groups. One, which was more substantial, was sent to Palo along the Lazio coast, while a second group including the command remained in Spoleto. The movement of the various divisions was given when the Anglo-Americans had broken through the Montecassino front and were advancing rapidly on Rome. Due to the confusion of the situation, it was not possible to organise an efficient line of connections, the same German commands on which we depended were falling back, so much so that at a certain point we realised that they had completely forgotten about us. My company from Spoleto received the order to move to Grosseto where the other two companies deployed in Palo were to fall back, the battalion command moved in the direction of Florence where we were all to regroup. Even the movement from Spoleto to Grosseto was difficult, it took several days also because it was practically impossible to move during the day because of the aerial machine gunfire. We moved in a few trucks but in the end only two arrived in Grosseto. The two companies that had to fall back to Grosseto had not been able to alert all their units scattered over a vast area and in the end the various groups fell back in isolation. In this chaotic situation, our officers were very busy, lingering as much as possible at various points of the front in order to make contact with as many of the isolated groups that were falling back without orders. On several occasions, having been overtaken by American vanguards, they had to fight their way through, even Captain Noweck tried his best not to leave any of us behind, so much so that he was wounded, albeit slightly, twice within a few days. In Grosseto, we had practically no vehicles left, as they had all been destroyed by enemy aviation. In small groups we started the retreat march to Florence where we would find the command post. After a few days of marching, I too arrived with the remains of my platoon in Florence where we were housed in a barracks. The stop in Florence continued for a few days then we were transferred by truck to Forlinpopoli where we stayed for about twenty days waiting for any groups that were falling back from the front, half of the battalion's personnel was missing.*

This instead is the account written by Corporal Antonio Stormi: '*31 May. Sudden order and departure for the front. The 3rd and 1st Company will deploy to Palo and south of Palo. Task: defence of the coast in case of a landing. The Anglo-Americans are approaching Rome. Unfortunately, ours will not be able to do much. Armed only with the old '91 rifles and a few* **Breda** *machine guns they have to wait for the Americans with the* **Shermans**. *5 June 1944. I leave with two trucks to pick up supplies and take them directly to the companies. After two days of waiting in Amelia I finally have the provisions and leave for Civitavecchia. I get as far as Orvieto then instead I have to go back to Montefiascone. Life is hard. Constantly during the day and night the planes fly over our heads. I have good luck. I have seen cars in front and behind mine, hit and burned. In Montefiascone I was saved almost by a miracle from a Spitfire barrage. I left again the next day for Orvieto. The British have occupied Rome. They are advancing fast. I don't make up my mind to leave. I always wait to see some of our cars.*

The *Oscha*. Adolfo S., battle name '**Hundred Guns**', **platoon commander of *Debica*.**

The last German vehicles with paratroopers pass by. I must decide if I don't want to remain a prisoner. Into the car and away. The 'Jabos' are always overhead. Every now and then they duck down and unload their bloody rosary beads. Burnt cars on the sides of the roads. Burnt bodies lie decomposed everywhere. In anguish I continue north. Not a trace of the battalion or our men. I think about their fate. Where will they be? Did they fight? Are they all dead or are they prisoners? Towards evening I meet by chance the car with Lieutenant Binder. He is tired and dejected. He tells me that the column has dispersed. He has no news of anyone. I am terribly depressed. Binder continues north. We make an appointment in Perugia. I also continue slowly. We pass a dusty road full of deep holes from bullet bursts. Putrid carrion lies on the road. Burning cars cloud the sky. A continuous, annoying ghibli-like dust cloud hovers over the road. It is excruciatingly hot. Before a bridge a column of 30 vehicles has been completely obliterated. It is night. Panzers pass by on their way south to stem the advance. I look up through the windscreen. Myriads of shining stars flicker across the sky and I think with heartfelt concern about the events. How will they stop the Anglo-American advance? Where? Where are the 'Debica' men? Still heading north. I am despondent but deep in my heart there is hope. Faith does not abandon me. We will hold. We will reattach. We will return soon, our dead brothers but for us alive and for Italy. And I see as confirmation to my thoughts an ever more distinct glimmer up there in the sky. There we draw the word Resurrection, the word Victory. I finally meet up with other 'Debica' comrades in Perugia. We have a few vehicles and the material we managed to take from Spoleto. There are only a few of us. Major Sassi and others, many others, are missing. We question ourselves with our eyes. But we don't have the courage to answer. Dead? Prisoners? Where are our brothers, our dear comrades? 7 June 1944. After a two-day halt 5 km from Perugia the 2nd Company leaves in the evening in the direction of Grosseto. We of the Battalion Command remain here as long as we can. We await the return of the trucks to take away at least part of the material. 13 June 1944. The lorries have not returned.

The Axis Forces

Young SS volunteer Claudio Misturelli in the *Debica* battalion.

We set off under a light drizzle. 14 June 1944. We pass by the post office to collect what is there for us. I find a telegram for me. My mother is seriously ill. I beg Lieutenant Tosatti to grant me leave. I finally leave alone for Trieste. Will I arrive in time? An obscure premonition tells me that I must hurry. One goes so slowly with the makeshift means. After two days I am in Florence. Here I stop for five days. I finally leave again for Bologna.

On 10 July, the battalion, reduced to around 200 men divided between two rifle companies, left Forlinpopoli bound for Pinerolo to rejoin the rest of the brigade, which had been assimilated to all intents and purposes into the *Waffen SS*, taking the name *Waffen Grenadier Brigade der SS*.

Notes

(1) According to some testimonies all Italian volunteers present were told that instead of returning to Italy, those who had joined would be sent to fight on other fronts and those who did not join would be sent back to prison camps. This was to avoid, as in fact happened, that many of the 'volunteers' had joined with the sole purpose of returning to Italy and then deserting.

(2) Then reduced to three.

(3) *1.Sturmbrigade*.

(4) This is what was reported on the arrival in Pinerolo by an SS volunteer: '*We arrived in Pinerolo today. A snowy, rainy day greeted us. It was cold. We pass through the town. The population looks at us surprised. There are more looks of hatred and pity than looks of joy. But what do we care?*'.

(5) The other units of the 1st Assault Brigade wore the red insignia, of the Waffen SS auxiliary units, until the early summer of 1944.

(6) Cantarella also briefly played the role of adjutant.

(7) This is the comment of an SS volunteer: '*We finally got the new uniforms. They are shiny cloth, parachutist type. At last we are somewhat decently dressed and almost look like a regular unit*'. According to the testimony of a second veteran, new uniforms, in the style of the German ones, were later distributed, made on the initiative of Captain Dal Dosso with flannel shirt and skier-style trousers.

(8) Sergeant Loris Ragoni: Poggibonsi 5.2.21 - 1st SS Battalion '*Debica*'. Ragoni has been a soldier since 1940 enlisted in the Italian navy as a telegrapher. During the African campaign he was embarked on the cruiser Trieste. On 1 October 1943, he voluntarily enlisted as a soldier in the *Waffen SS* and from 22 February 1944, he was part of the 1st SS Battalion '*Debica*' Company as squad commander. During his training, he demonstrated an exemplary sense of duty. During the attack conducted on 21 March 1944 by the 1a Company against the enemy-occupied heights west of Torre Pellice, he led an assault group against an enemy observation post. Heavy enemy fire pinned the men down to the point where they could not retreat. To set an example to his men Ragoni continued to stand up to the enemy despite the intense fire, eventually managing to penetrate the building occupied by the partisans and kill four of them. Ragoni himself was seriously wounded by machine-gun fire in several places in his stomach, dying shortly after due to the severity of his wounds. During the operations in Val Pellice he particularly

distinguished himself in the excellent leadership of his unit. Despite being seriously wounded in the head and chest he remained at his men's side until the enemy positions were conquered.

(9) Lance Corporal Roberto Pizzi: Stradella 26.3.1920 - 1st SS Battalion '*Debica*'. Pizzi has been a soldier since 1940 and took part in the Albanian and Greek campaigns as an artilleryman. After the capitulation of Italy, on 1 October 1943 he applied as a volunteer to fight against the enemies of New Europe. From 22 February 1944, he was enlisted in the 2nd a Company of the 1st Btg./1st Regiment as commander of a rifle squad. Pizzi distinguished himself during the training period for his dedication in carrying out his services and for his camaraderie spirit. During the attack conducted by the 2a Company together with the Battalion on Villar Pellice on 21 March 1944, the company was hit by intense automatic weapons fire from the mountains to the right of the road. Pizzi was hit by shrapnel in the head but nevertheless led his group forward. By his own example, he led his group to the capture of an enemy stronghold and the capture of a machine gun. As further pockets of resistance prevented him from ascending the valley, he gave further orders to go on the assault and thus succeeded in penetrating into the heart of the enemy ranks. His heroism was thus sanctioned by his death in the battle.

(10) Corporal Giovanni Fois: Arben 9.3.18 - SS '*Debica*' Battalion. Corporal Fois, during an attack on rebel positions in Val Pellice, was employed as an order bearer under the company commander. Commanded to carry important orders he had to cross a stretch of road in the open under intense enemy machine-gun fire. On this occasion, Fois was shot in the stomach and seriously wounded. For his sense of duty and spirit of sacrifice he was an excellent example for his comrades.

(11) It was Emanuele Artom. After the war, Captain Dal Dosso was accused of the ill-treatment of Artom, who was later killed, and was tried by the extraordinary assize court of Turin. Dal Dosso, who was sentenced to 30 years, could not have taken part in the interrogation and torture because he had been seriously injured on 21 March. This is the defence brief sent from Brazil by the officer: '*I was a captain, commander of the 2nd Company of the 1st Battalion of the 1st Italian SS Regiment from February 1944 to 25 April 1945. On 19 April 1951 I was sentenced by the Turin Court of Assizes to life imprisonment, a sentence later commuted to 30 years. This sentence, as well as for various charges of round-ups carried out in Val Pellice and Valli di Lanzo, was particularly provoked by the killing of three captured partisans. After 25 April I was interned at the American concentration camp in Coltano, I then lived in Albese (Como) until August 1947 then I was housed at a religious confraternity in central Italy until November 1948. From November 1948 to November 1952 I was in the Spanish Foreign Legion in Tahmina (Melilla) in Spanish Morocco. Since 1953 I have been in Brazil. My war service during the time of the Italian Social Republic is no different in its characteristics from my service as an officer in previous campaigns, I mean in the 1915-18 Italian-Austrian war, the Italian and Macedonian front, the 1919 Libyan campaign, the 1935-40 campaign to conquer the empire, and the 1940-43 campaign in Greece and the Balkans. During these campaigns I also earned two decorations for military valour, one in 1917 and the other in 1937. I declare that I fought as a partisan, but not with the idea of fighting the Italian army, in which case I would have been very poorly represented, but with the conviction of fighting a rebel against the laws of his country, abusively armed, without a uniform and therefore not military uniform, flaunting non-Italian insignia, red flag and hammer and sickle and hammer, and who in most cases attacked first and when he could, treacherously. The only time I had a firefight with the Val Pellice partisans was on 21 March 1944 when, with the unit marching from Torre Pellice towards Bobbio Pellice, I was attacked on the road with rifles and mortars and seriously wounded. I do not know the three partisans who were shot because I was in hospital and did not learn of the fact until after the trial, I have never made any arrests in Luserna or elsewhere, if at times I had to send someone from Luserna to the Pinerolo command it was to comply with a similar request from the command. I never tortured any partisans; those partisans who surrendered with weapons in their hands were either voluntarily enlisted in our unit or sent to the command, all my actions were always military in character and I never acted as a police officer. In the course of my department's military operations it could happen that soldiers took possession of some valuable object and when this came to my knowledge, the object was returned to its owner. I was sent to Luserna San Giovanni twice; the first time at the end of February 1944, after an officer of my regiment, Lieutenant Hafner, an Italian officer from Alto Adige, had been treacherously murdered in the village, and the second time on my return from the war operations for the defence of Rome, in July. During these two periods I had three men murdered within the village, one non-commissioned officer and two troop men, buried next to Lieutenant Hafner in that cemetery. I never ordered reprisals. With regard to acts carried out against specific individuals such as Artom etc., I declare that I have never heard of them, nor have I arrested them, still less tortured or killed them. I believe I can state with absolute certainty that in the Luserna area, at least as far as I am concerned, the only dead were from my battalion. I believe that the accusations against me are due to personal error, whether intentional or accidental. I have nothing further to add*'.

(12) Born in Villaverla (Vi) on 3.3.18.

(13) Born in Villetta Barrea (Aq) on 18.1.18. In some documents referred to as Gianfranco Selvitze.

(14) Order of the Command of the 14(a) Army to the Command of the 92a Infantry Division of 29 May, according to which *the division can count on the assignment of a new battalion of the* SS-Sturmbrigade 'Italia' *in the coming days. This battalion is to be deployed in a low-risk sector of the front.*

(15) Marshal Walter Morini: Reggio Emilia 27.6.1915 - SS *'Debica'* Battalion. Morini took part in the Abyssinian War where he was decorated with the Bronze Medal for valour shown in battle. He then took part in the Libyan and Tunisian campaigns where he was twice seriously wounded. On these fronts too, for the courage he showed, he was again decorated and promoted to the rank of sergeant. From September 1943 to January 1944, he did a training period in Germany and from February 1944 he was platoon commander in an SS infantry battalion. He took part in the fighting along the Nettuno bridgehead, in Rome and in the area of Lake Bolsena. Here he particularly distinguished himself for bravery on 2 and 5 June 1944. Several times he found himself surrounded with his platoon by Anglo-American vanguards, managing with very few losses to avoid the annihilation of his unit. At the head of his platoon, he led the assault on an enemy high post where prisoners and considerable amounts of material were captured.

(16) Marshal Enrico Vicentini: Verona, 15.4.15 - SS *'Debica'* Battalion. Team commander, he was sent to guard an advanced point on the Rome front. He held the position despite being overrun by enemy tanks. After being ordered to fall back, he skilfully led his squad through enemy-occupied territory and under intense heavy weapons fire. He managed to bring his squad back to our positions without losses. Vicentini showed calmness and confidence as a squad commander on this occasion, managing to keep his men compact despite the intense enemy fire.

(17) Marshal Fernando Vasquez: La Spezia, 19.10.10 - SS *'Debica'* Battalion. Vasquez was seconded to the command of the German Liaison Officer. Both at night and during the day he was often commanded to carry orders and news between the command and the troops on the line. During these missions he was attacked several times by rebel nuclei. On one occasion, despite being seriously wounded, he managed with superhuman effort to bring important news to the command. He distinguished himself on other occasions for his indomitable spirit and uncommon strength of will.

(18) Corporal Umberto Lucarelli: Turin, 8.8.10 - SS *'Debica'* Battalion. Corporal Lucarelli carried out the service of order bearer, often finding himself passing under enemy fire to carry his orders and messages. While returning to company command, he realised that enemy tanks had broken through the front line and were threatening the entire unit with encirclement. Thanks to his information, almost the entire division was able to disengage and safely reach the new front line. Lucarelli distinguished himself on several occasions for his courage and disregard for danger.

(19) Born in Ravenna on 12.6.1920.

Bibliography

Leonardo Sandri, "*il battaglione SS 'Debica', SS-Freiwilligen Bataillon 'Debica': una documentazione*" Edito in Proprio

Sergio Corbatti, Marco Nava, "*Sentire-Pensare-Volere, Storia della Legione SS italiana*", Ritter edizioni

Massimiliano Afiero, "*Italiani nella Waffen-SS*", Associazione Culturale Ritterkreuz

Photographic references: the photos in the article, where not otherwise specified, come from the collection of Sergio Corbatti and Marco Nava.

SS-Unterscharführer Egon Christophersen

by Antonio Guerra

SS-Unterscharführer **Egon Christophersen.**

Egon Christophersen, *Unterscharführer* in the *Waffen-SS* during World War II, was the first of three Danish volunteers to be decorated with the Knight's Cross of the Iron Cross. He was born on 8 February 1919 in Strøby, Denmark. From the age of seven, he attended the local school in Strøby and then worked on an experimental farm from the age of fourteen with his three brothers. With the start of the war, Christophersen joined the National Socialist Workers' Party of Denmark, shortly afterwards becoming a member of its armed militia, the *Storm Afdeling*. On 7 April 1941, he joined the *Waffen-SS*. He was then transferred to Graz to complete his basic training with the reserve battalion of the *SS-Regiment Der Führer*. After completing his training, he was assigned to the *11th Kompanie* of the *SS-Regiment Nordland* of *SS-Division Wiking* in August 1941, but was soon after transferred to the *9th Kp./Nordland*. When the division was transferred to the Eastern Front, Christophersen was again transferred to another company, this time the *2.Kp./Nordland*. In May 1942, he was promoted to *Sturmmann*. During the fighting in the Caucasus, he was wounded in both thighs and was evacuated to a military hospital in September 1942. After his convalescence, he was transferred to the *SS-Regiment Westland*'s depot battalion in Graz. Christophersen remained in Graz until February 1943, when he returned to his division, the *Wiking*, which had meanwhile been transformed into a new armoured grenadier division. He was decorated with the Iron Cross Second Class for distinction in the fighting in the Caucasus and was promoted to *Unterscharführer*.

In May 1943, Christophersen was transferred to the new SS *Nordland* Division, formed around *SS-Regiment Norland*, which was quartered in Grafenwohr. He was then assigned to the *7.Kompanie* of the new *SS-Panzergrenadier Regiment 24* 'Danmark', composed mainly of Danish volunteers. After completing its training, this unit was sent to Croatia to be engaged against the Titine partisan formations. Egon's brother Viggo, also enlisted in the *Waffen-SS*, was killed during this same period. The *SS-Division Nordland* together with the SS *Nederland* Brigade, united in the *III.(Germ.)SS-Panzer-Korps*, were transferred between December 1943 and January 1944 to the Leningrad front in the Oranienbaum sector.

On the Narva Front

Motorised elements of the SS *Nordland* division in a Croatian village, summer 1943 (NARA).

Grenadiers of the *Danmark* regiment on a defensive position, summer 1944 (NARA).

After the retreat from the Leningrad front, the units of the *III.(Germ.)SS-Pz.Korps* were stationed on the Narva front as early as February 1944. The defensive fighting lasted for months, until the spring and early summer. Christophersen's *7.Kp./Danmark* was entrenched in the area south of Narva and east of Kreenholm, next to the district of Dolgaya Niva. These positions were attacked by Soviet units as early as 20 May and in the following days. On 7 June 1944, the Soviets launched an attack against the *Sonnenschein* outpost defended by the 7th Danmark, causing numerous losses among the Danish volunteers. The remnants of the company, under the command of Danish *SS-Ustuf*. Leo Madsen, somehow managed to repel this first attack. Five days later, the Soviets attacked again, being preceded by a heavy bombardment of their artillery. The Sonnenschein sector thus found itself completely isolated. The Soviet artillerymen employed smoke shells that covered the entire landscape in an artificial fog. The clouds of smoke even reached the command post of the *II./Danmark* at Dolgaja-Niva. A few minutes later, *SS-Ustuf*. Madsen, launched a rocket bright, to call for help, as the remains of his

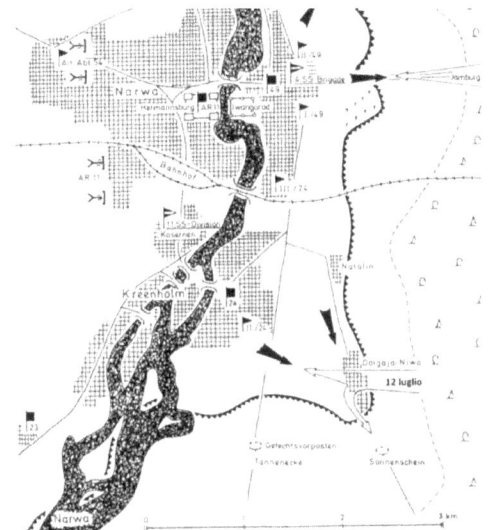

Dislocation of the German forces on the Narva bridgehead. Bottom right, the *Danmark* positions with the Sonnenschein outpost.

Company were totally surrounded at Sonnenschein. He knew very well that he could not hold the position for long, so he decided to attempt a breakthrough manoeuvre to join his battalion at Dolgaja-Niva. But by then it was too late, the Soviet grip had tightened firmly around them. Under the cover of fog and the roar of explosions, the Soviet soldiers again attacked the positions of the 7. Two platoon commanders fell at the head of their men, *SS-Ustuf.* Johannes Koopmann and *SS-Ustuf.* Arne Michaelsen. Only a group of about ten men, led by *SS-Uscha.* Egon Christophersen, continued to hold, on the north wing of the position. The rocket fired by Madsen at the beginning of the attack was seen from the observation post of the *Nordland* artillery regiment.

A *Nordland* machine-gun squad in advanced position, 1944.

The guns went into action and sent a deluge of fire over the area east of Dolgaja-Niva, where the Soviets had massed their troops. In the meantime, at least two hundred Soviet infantrymen had already launched themselves through the open breach and managed to gain more ground. Other Soviet divisions emerged from the forests and launched themselves against the position already under attack. The guns of the *SS-Ostubaf.* Karl's guns adjusted their fire well, literally pulverising the Soviet infantry, which disappeared in the smoke and explosions. But more enemy forces arrived soon afterwards and it seemed that nothing could stop the Soviet units, who continued to attack, despite the heavy losses they suffered: the Soviets now seemed to be in control of the *Sonnenschein* outpost and were also pushing into Dolgaja-Niva, where house-to-house fighting was taking place. The group, led by Christophersen, was still holding, although it was totally surrounded.

Danmark soldiers in the shelter of a trench on the Narva front, summer 1944.

Grenadiers *of Danmark.*

The Norwegian *SS-Hstuf.* Erik Lärum, commander of the 13. /*Danmark*, equipped with 150mm howitzers, had observed the fighting around Sonnenschein from his forward position and, seeing the seriousness of the situation, decided to abandon his howitzers momentarily to relieve the SS grenadiers. Leading a battle group, comprising his artillerymen and the grenadiers of the two heavy companies of the *II.* and *III.* In addition, Lärum requested mortar and artillery support from the divisional command: all the guns and heavy weapons in the sector concentrated their fire on the Soviet positions around Dolgaja-Niva. Completely submerged under a veritable firestorm, the Soviet soldiers were forced to take cover to avoid being killed. Immediately after the artillery action, a counter-attack was launched with all available forces: the *SS-Hstuf.* Herbert Meyer arrived with part of his company, the 9. /*Danmark*, participating in the assault against Dolgaja-Niva, while other elements of the 8. and 16. /*Danmark*, arrived as reinforcements together with two *StuG III* assault guns. *The Danmark* grenadiers arrived shortly afterwards between the trenches, where the survivors of the Soviet attack had taken refuge, took some 40 prisoners and regained the lost ground. Soon afterwards, the connection was established with their comrades from the *7.Kompanie*, grouped around *SS-Uscha.* Christophersen.

Danmark Grenadiers in the shelter of a trench prepare to launch an attack against Soviet positions, summer 1944.

The Danish sergeant had not waited for the arrival of reinforcements, to launch counter-attacks with his handful of grenadiers to the south and north of his position, thus managing to break through the encirclement. *The SS-Hstuf.* Heinz Hämel, who had moved to the front line, joined the Danish NCO in the trenches, whom he knew very well, when he had been in command of his company, to personally decorate him with the Iron Cross of First Class and later recommend him for the Knight's Cross, the first Danish volunteer to receive it, which was officially awarded to him on 11 July 1944.

Left, *SS-Uscha*. Christophersen immediately after being decorated with the Iron Cross First Class. In the photo on the right, again the *SS-Uscha*. Christophersen (second from right) with other Danish volunteers decorated with the Iron Cross Second Class.

Only three Danes received the Knight's Cross during the Second World War, the other two being *SS-Ostuf.* Søren Kam and *SS-Ostuf.* Johannes Hellmers. Egon Christophersen survived the war and returned to live in Køge in Denmark. He worked in the *Hansen* factory in Ørum for over thirty years. He died on 15 January 1988.

Two photos of the *SS-Uscha*. Egon Christophersen with the Knight's Cross.

Another signed photo of Christophersen.   Under licence in Denmark.

www.ingramcontent.com/pod-product-compliance
Lightning Source LLC
LaVergne TN
LVHW081452060526
838201LV00050BA/1777